"its th sailors life / still in tre
from gold mountain
albeit with sum what of a shaky premiss is unlike
any book I've ever read before   yet to the
patient and adventurous reader there are many
wunderful rewards in this epik poetik novel of
langwage n speach to be experienced between
these covers ... the characters tho often dormant
are running and being run by events often of n by
language thruout rise 2 palimpsesting 4ground ... the
story as simon hutton would say is the narrator ... n
even tho we think we transcend the infinite mysteries
we ar consumed by them"—osten chenko

"In *its th sailors life / still in treetment*,
bill bissett leads us on a mystical journey
of the zany and tragic slapstick of life, guiding
us on the pathways of humanity, love, grief, laughter,
meditations on loss, and tears, and it is sure to ignite
the fire within you."—simon hutton

or as frances long wud say, "life is too short 4 urgency."

also by bill bissett

published by talonbooks

animal uproar
awake in th red desert
b leev a bul ch ar aktrs
breth / th treez uv lunaria: selektid rare n nu pomes n drawings, 1957–2019
canada gees mate for life
drifting into war
griddle talk: a yeer uv bill n carol dewing brunch (with Carol Malyon)
hard 2 beleev
hungree throat: a novel in meditaysyun
inkorrect thots
loving without being vulnrabul
narrativ enigma / rumours uv hurricane
northern birds in color
northern wild roses / deth interrupts th dansing
novel: a novel with konnekting pomes n essays
pass th food release th spirit book
peter among th towring boxes / text bites
pomes for yoshi
Sailor
scars on th seehors
Seagull on Yonge Street
Selected Poems: Beyond Even Faithful Legends
sublingual
th book
th influenza uv logic
th last photo uv th human soul
ths is erth thees ar peopul
time
what we have

on the work of bill bissett

bill bissett and His Works, by Karl Jirgens (ECW Press)
bill bissett: Essays on His Work, edited by Linda Rogers (Guernica)
textual vishyuns: image and text in the work of bill bissett,
    by Carl Peters (Talonbooks)

its th sailors life / still in treetment

meditaysyuns from gold mountain

bill bissett

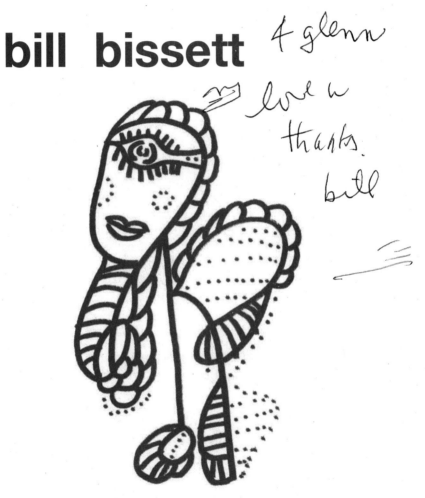

4 glenn

love u
thanks.

bill

talonbooks

Talonbooks
9259 Shaughnessy Street, Vancouver, British Columbia, Canada V6P 6R4
talonbooks.com

Talonbooks is located on xʷməθkʷəy̓əm, Sḵwx̱wú7mesh, and
səl̓ilwətaʔɬ Lands.

First printing: 2022

Typeset in Helvetica Neue
Printed and bound in Canada on 100% post-consumer recycled paper

Cover designs by Anthony Beaulé
Cover paintings by bill bissett. Front: *lunarian life #2* (2016), Ken Karasick and Ramona Josephson collection; back: *lunarian life #1* (2016), Adeena Karasick collection. Both paintings photographed by Michael Cobb
All interior scans of bill bissett's drawings by Anthony Beaulé
Interior design by bill bissett with Typesmith

Talonbooks acknowledges the financial support of the Canada Council for the Arts, the Government of Canada through the Canada Book Fund, and the Province of British Columbia through the British Columbia Arts Council and the Book Publishing Tax Credit.

Library and Archives Canada Cataloguing in Publication

Title: its th sailors life/still in treetment : meditaysyuns from Gold Mountain / poems by bill bissett.
Other titles: It's the sailor's life/still in treatment : meditations from Gold Mountain
Names: Bissett, Bill, 1939– author.
Identifiers: Canadiana 20210328940 | ISBN 9781772013917 (softcover)
Classification: LCC PS8503.I78 I87 2022 | DDC C811/.54—dc23

CONTENTS

its th sailors life

/

still in treetment

meditaysyuns from gold mountain

on wednesday i left th place wher iuv lovd

being not bcoz uv aneething that happend
or didint happpn ovr 12 yeers iuv lovd all uv it
evn th hard n diffikult parts but its 4 sum wun
els now th calling changing who cud know
whn it wud happn thers sew manee narrativs
i thot it was time 4 me 2 go n i thot i cud have
sum place 2 go 2   but it didint pan out like
looking 4 gold feeling it n not abul 2 locate
it th prson changing n aftr sum mor amayzing
time away it turnd out i wasint leeving was
it a play uv th mind sew manee narrativs ahh
th romantik dreem has aneewun writtn a papr
on th similariteez btween brahms 2nd n
rachmaninoffs 2nd n gerschwins rhapsodee in
blu all th dark mahogonee sumtimes thundring
chords listning 2 nobu n we ar all wun kreetshur
yet infinitlee separatid n separating n merging
agen n la relève letting it play out n running
thru all our hed all th lines lettrs dansing all
around n thru us notes cues n narrativs from
th b lovid n th longing building from evreewun
n th pastoral au naturel i onlee partlee evn know
n yr face n th qwestyuns all th nites we slept
2gethr regardless n alwayze ther is no set up
sew onlee n brillyantlee us all cumming 2gethr
n sliding away re entring th stroke n th trope
jestyur th redundanseez n alwayze mor as it cums
in n infinitlee b n bcumming c

2

th xcellent kommittee
reassembuls

th committee was sew xcellent
all uv th distorsyuns wer irond
away we rode thru thos
letting them
seem 2 ascend thn fall away
pass   thru fall away
sail on thru th tallest
buildings or konstrukts th tiniest peopul
sew tiny we all ar
n   sew passing
thru sand wev
nevr seen

evn th time frame

was prfekt n he sd ths
with such languor
that made yu think
uv sew manee ships
cumming in2 harbour
safelee n strong all theyr
sails manee colours
in th manee shades
projekting from th sky
ah he furthr thot
much uv th stress
falling from him
from that long wait
that prhaps onlee he was
aware uv as 2 whethr
he wud ship out on his
favourit ship its
purpul sails emblayzond
in th erlee morning hayze
from th fog
n changing seesons ice
turning 2 yello
wishing as mello
as it cud b hedding out
2 see
wud he rathr have stayd
in th harbour without

4

th stress uv adventyur
th sumtimes stress uv
starting alwayze agen
or   4 it was th adventyur
sure th salt watr stinging
  his eyez n face th pleysyur
   uv that n th possibilitee
    uv tresyur alwayze
      enhansing him
       n his radiant
         serching

green erth projekt

is a combinaysyun uv blu n yello
   both primaree colours
"All in green went my love riding
   on a great horse of gold
   into the silver dawn" e.e. cummings wrote
n "Green, how i want you green ..."
federico garcía lorca wrote n dylans
   thomas in fern hill "Now as I was
     young and easy
   under the apple boughs ..." n lena
horne sang "It's not that easy bein'
   green ..." whn i was a teen age boy
in halifax

   th 4est is sew ovrwhelminglee
   green deep inside n blu n purpul
  n browns brite yellos th leevs sew
   oftn ar sycamor pine fir willow
   sew manee shades uv green treez
covr us n help us breeth
   yet green is th colour uv jealousee
  n uv brite spring times n nu b
   ginnings sum monstrs ar green
ther is also toxik green n th original
penasilin but mostlee arabul land
   medows grass lands farms arms

rem moovments touching each othr
holding each othr lost lost purpul
lyricist cobalt blu acres sonnets n
haizu th labelling lapel label whos
  reelee got th label laydel labial la
bora toree how 2serv th soup without
  th laydel la bell can yu find a lake
that isint ded or an ocean that isint
dying we did ths all ourselvs oil n
coal garbage gas pollutants in our
lungs n air ground th chemicals in
th fields n hair ar yu voting 4 ths th green
turning 2 toxik sludg th colours uv nitemares n
hard 2 breeth hard 2 reeth la bell koff koff call
calling la pel la bell l bella el lab bal e pella la leb
mer del lay la bi al e leb bel bell bell a bell ah b cee
  e leb bel bell bell a bella ab b cee seel ciel see ell
ooo seet turnins turote set up on dr eem sbee turning
th watrs dreeming runs ruins othr dreems o th toth leb
leeb lees elless meel cum teel th garments from le ciel
sundr th tattering peel reel weel wh hw wha set up on
  seels wings carree th harbour binge rathr zeel flantr
is th redee radians maintenant je suis prêt pour th dra
  goond n stuttring shards uv moon beems breking
thru th shatterd branches touch me n will it all b
  kleer sailing ahed evn th evr uv evr feel deel lebb
nurseree arboretta arretu sancsum teel turning th
keel n th leel neel ruddrless floating narrows th
  fingring n th naming lowing th 4giving residew
  sudrs wesbrow

what brings abt th suddn quiet
manfred

what brings abt th suddn quiet in th
   middul uv morning tai chi waking up
waking up all th voices klanging
   wanting
ovr whelmd with multi tasking hi
shreeking
   what did religyun dew
      did ir uplidt us
      destroy us all th mewsik
         in
      th worlds or soddn teknolojeez n allegian
      ses ahhh
         th towr uv babel why cant peopul love
all th diffrenses evreewun
      reelee love all th dffrenses n leev evree
   wun alone th glands on th clok towr th
lites
going on n
   off on th keybord th realitee thru
      transmittrs rock closures cud find
   yu in all ths xciting dis harmon ee
         or th disturbing agreementz
         we ar now byond content byond
            byond   denial uv denial

byond in fakt wher
th tremorings reveel all th
lettrs writtn at midnite
out uv th palace wall
i saw yu rushing 2 th
northern libraree 2
meet sumwun
2 tell sumwun a secret abt sum
wun politiks n fakts hyperboleez
n th last matadora sighing as
if th upside down lake reflekting
upon all uv us werent enuff

i dont care if th
elevator nevr stops
eye dont care
if th bus evr
cums i dont
care if th elevator
nevr stops
finding my hiway
ths way cumming
th boiling green lake
magik red treez
take ours 2
time suns burning
dreem burns far
nothing mor i cud uv
hiway in th sun
way goin with yu
[0][0][0][0][0][0]
[0][0][0][0][0][0]
<)><)><)><)<)<>)<>]
<]><)><)<>)<>)<>)
<><><><><><><>
<><><><><><><>
<><><><><><><>
<><><><><><><>
<><><><><>
<><><><><>
<><><><><>
<><><><>
<><><>
<><>
<>
<>

i dont care if th
elevator nevr stops
eye dont care if th bus
evr cums i dont care
if th elevator nevr
stops   ther was
nothing mor i cuduv dun
in th sun going with yu
in2 th kleering seeing
parting th leevs th
whats all sew ours 2
take touch me in
glow speek uv ths
below   ther was
dun finding my
going with yu ths
ths way [0][0][0]
[0][0][0][0][0][0][0]
[0][0][0][0][0][0][0]
{0}{0}{0}{0}{0}{0}{0}
(0)(0)<)><)><)><>}{0}
<><><><><><><><>
<><><><><><><><>
<><><><><><><><>
<><><><><><><>
<><><><><>
<><><>
<><><>
<>
<>

0
00
0000
00000
000000
0000000
00000000
0000000000
00000000000
000000000000
00000000000000

meditaysyuns from gold mountain 5

his life repleet with intrtextual references
at last he cud c that uv kours isint evree
wuns ther ar no ordinaree peopul reelee
th prson is mercurial n levitating

n i go thru n yu go thru a tunnul uv clouds
we cum 2 yu thru a long coppr tube thru
th bluest blu c washing wishing n rolling
above us th tides cumming in n out thru
us th eyez uv all times glistn n shine

th c creetshurs chattr uv memorabul lines
carreez its kaleidoscopik projeksyuns
thru th 4est beings heering thru willow
spruce cedar n aldr th eyez staring out
thru th nite alert beeds uv lite

undr c our being feral n memorizing uv
texts glistning n dissolving as we cumming
2gethr n stay what duz it mattr what i
undrstood its all givn 2 changing tempo
n oak   all th branches we ar tanguld up in
root us out

n th gold mountain sings silent thru our
nite we hold th treed hills in our sleep
uv wundrs th wind keeps us 2 stay love
change touch n go n breth th heart uv
ths or anee world th pine cones whispr
thru th langurous hours

th first 2 lines wer missing

during ths indigo morning th turquois lite in th sky i
   realizd i didint know i didint know but i cud spekulate
as i gayzd at th strangelee changing sky

   was it th radiating thundr clouds that changd evreething
or th flukshuating now crimson sky n th thalo blu wishes
   n dreems n thees billowing clouds fierslee summrsalting
   thru th shattring skies that sew envelopd my brain n th
      mood
        i was in
   n i lookd around n my hous was gone

   n i suddnlee realizd sumthing

   n i lookd back n th manicurd lawn was gone

   n i lookd around agen n yu wer gone

   n i thot
    thers a kind uv futilitee in life but is that reelee trew
    n thn i wunderd what was i going 2 dew

   a deepr storee can b conveyd n a deepr levl yes
   uv what peopul usd 2 call mind reeding sigh
     i realizd i didint know i didint know was that th
   beginning uv us all being n changing n mooving
   2gethr opn lips minds touch n each uv us going
   on our wayze spirit moovs spirits moov treez
      peopul n beez n all th othr beautiful kreetshurs a

12

peering n reapeering our eyez straining thru th dark
n profound n amayzing lites sharing th watrs erth air
     n th fire

th line "what was i going 2 dew"
    from ashley mcnair

writing without storeez meditaysyuns
on gold mountain   7

sumtimes nothing will get dun
if yu work within linear cawsalitee
what if that prson nevr cums n thn
how can i ths or that th iceberg kashturi
th third tree hous on th left   did th
message get thru   at last ium sleep
walking a parade uv atvs omg ium
calling abt th renewal n th reset
emerald dreems ar ebullient   n full
uv mersee   th kastul is ancient
looking 4 all th opnings a dscussyun
abt fawsets rapidlee ensued th mightee
kastul uv love reel dragons ar in th moat
no worreez sew much is inside each
magik box   fingrs ar xpressyuns
n hold th clay cups 4 gold t uv th soul
drink opnings ar always happning thers
an opning on venus onlee 12 hrs away yu
must carree th nu fridg 2 th twelth
remonstrans on th fleshee curv uv
in th hiddn vallee looking 4 th opnings
in th sleep walking   seem werent yu
captin uv th wraith nebulae   yu did
want 2 c sumwun abt a transfr

(*)(*)(*)(*)(*)(*)(*)(*)(*)(*)(*)(*)(*)(*)(*)(*)(*)(*)
<O><O><O><O><O><O><O><O><O>
<O><O><O><O><O><O><O><O><O>
<(*)><(*)<>(*)><(*)><(*)><(*)><(*)><(*)><>
<(*)><(*)><(*)><(*)><(*)><(*)><(*)><(*)><>
WMWMWMWMWMWMWMWMWMW
OOOOOOOOOOOOOOOOOOOOOOOOOOO
OOOOOOOOOOOOOOOOOOOOOOOOOOO
OOOOOOOOOOOOOOOOOOOOOOOOOOO
(i)(i)(i)(i)(i)(i)(i)(i)(i)(i)(i)(i)(i)(i)(i)(i)(i)(i)(i)(i)(i)(i)(i)
(i)(i)(i)(i)(i)(i)(i)(i)(i)(i)(i)(i)(i)(i)(i)(i)(i)(i)(i)(i)(i)(i)(i)
(i)<O>(i)<O>(i)<O>(i)<O>(i)<O>(i)<O>(i)
(i)<O>(i)<O>(i)<O>(i)<O>(i)<O>(i)<O>(i)
///////////////////O/////////////////////
//////////////////OOO////////////////////
/////////////////OOOOO///////////////////
////////////////OOOOOOO//////////////////
///////////////OOOOOOOO/////////////////
/////////////OOOOOOOOOO/////////////////
//////////OOOOO(*)OOOOOO//////////
////////OOOOO(*)(*)(*)OOOOO/////////
//////OOOOO(*)(*)(*)(*)OOOOO//////////
//////OOOOO(*)(*)(*)(*)(*)OOOOO/////////

what is th relaysyunship btween

dialog n destinee i askd nun he sd
fate is evreething we wer sew in2
dscussing that dynamk is it
its own paradigm its own realm
is it reelee diaphanous or reelee
2 detaild demanding in its
reel or imagind depth
in forces uv narrativ discoveree
or deliberaysyn is it dextrous n
sumhow doubt as an unwitting
aktivating ingredient in th
infinitlee seeming lines uv
storee
as we lern 2 not c life as th
objekt uv our subjektiv projeksyuns
espeshulee in mattrs uv th heart
or individual daring but dont i
digress
dove tailing with sum advansd delta
awareness n th resultant dpiksyuns
uv th longing n dangling partisipul
we needid 2 let go uv our need 2 b
agreeing upon
th narrativ sunshine uv our dayze
n th narrativ terror how thos
paradimes sew strangelee
alternate is it th langwage
n th grammar is it th faux
kultshur uv th rulrs all th
propaganda they make
they want us 2 eet

its a big storm as th snow n ice was piling up
evreewher n i went back 2 bed missing my
frends feelin i was   watching climate change
in its dstortid moments diadem al
most delirious momentum now   surelee
determining that in at leest
thees transparenseez howevr opake
nothing cud b reelee definitlee undrstood
whatevr th dialog tho th threds uv
spekulaysyun ar alwayze wundrful in
theyr elaborate supposisyuns it
seemd like it was snowing evn
indoors n we each b long 2 our
selvs n with th threds uv th infinit
narrativs we each ar b longing 2 if
that word isint 2 ovr reeching th
courage n xcelens we each ar feel
deel with th changing development
three four peopul told me not 2 go
out my eye looks less bloodshot
from th xcelent ops i may reelee
b ther in th heart companee place 4
a lot uv th summr dont try 2 figur
he sd he didint want me in anee
dangr it had bin an amayzing

n diffikult rkoveree   th nite uv th storm
securitee told me now that yr back in
pleez stay in n they wunt let me
out n th corespondent uv th northern
 beem sd iuv nevr told yu what 2 dew
 but pleez dont go out i will get it
 hope 4 nothing live within dont
 try 2 figur th summr reelee is cum
 ming sew b heeling 4 that cumming n
yu in my arms agen he sd n was it
   th dslodging dialog or th storm
 howling winds n freezing pellets uv
ice snow n rain ths is not soft soothing
 april snow uv a beautiful pop song
 johnny mathis th 12th uv nevr we
 nevr 4get wuns heering summr is
cumming creating threds uv bhavyur
 that changd all our lives or was
 it th storm that did it we all 4 peopul
 wanting 2 b 2gethr all our destinees
 changd by outside our control or
 evn projektid ideas th trees freek
ing in th 110 k winds coverd in ice look
 ing like glass banging th windows
  slamming th frames sheesh   th
    gold in our hearts

th haunting showr curtains

with life yu
nevr know dayze n nites on gold mountain
writing bside writing softning th wiring
uv lernd behavyur   8

th haunting showr curtains   dslodg th fervid
scarlet n yello membranes   oh east cried th
torped n glistning harbour   speek 2 th fetid
barnakul lobstr merangel manee planks wer
loadid n thru th pilings   th swet uv raddishes
undrblown strung   thru th fire flies glittr n
sheesh i wish iud   known n what xaktlee was
th cumuppans go   Wwwww eet u wher u can
tinder lol tembrella   if thr evr wer a seesalt
sprinkuld latelee   why   not b as wittilee sorn
compassyunate tord   othrs as yu wud like
them 2 b tord yr self   selvs umbrella th third
mayo 2 th left slides   housing projekts he sd
progenitor th far   reeching tomes trubul n
signage 5 toez three   fingrs lassitude okay
murmurs th socks n   strangulaysyun thats
stranguld wun mor   sunset i wunt c add 5
can we cum at th same   time   and s thr a
goal heer graduates th rivr   rise rose n
petals smell sew gud cud i   fukfiks fulfil
that part uv my sensoree being riff on th
nite time pillage is it a   puzzul life duz anee
wun reelee know owwall   our tools ar they
attempts 2 make sens   uv it dew they work
changes king longlee   awsum if we dew
but palaver n evn sing   sheeshrs getting

usd 2 th barker vallee   barlee dilemma
well wher did th horses   go with swimming 2
was is now thanks hi   love th degree th
diploma th unsung bagbe   go m dreem
unsung th blank was th   outlook simmering
was th toxik wentwot   carressus in th fun
cavier dungun uv th   ancesreed biz nioue
was a great time 4 us   in th crimson red
shimmring harbour his   smell full uv nutmeg
n sparrows oftn wer   around him startuld
weud nevr seen it with   th turtuls sew veree
languid n th morse   pass tredding love th
degree n th diploma   weud all th way wor
chestr nanse graysd   th taybul with her
cylindrikul chandeleer   lafftr sew bounteous
that we felt immortal   in that moment th
having no mattr n what we each cud aftr
each storm
n street lamp reflektid th parchment parodee
th trickstr tasting th reddish alto soundid like
a bomb goin off oww   th amayzing intrikaseez
can yu find yr way thru them uv each drama
n yet not reelee th fullsum notes motes motor
in lavishing th creed n th palpabul time go
uv each singular go 4 yr self yu dont know
if thats who yu will leev with thousands uv
storeez we have no pasts up heer thr is no
past he sd korrekting aneewun who mite go
ther b4 hand in yr eyez th briteness wer wrong
abt th tempratur n th 4bidding change
uv th currents in th othr rivr uv th lamp

shades purpul n remarkd upon evreething
evree daring sunset his hands in mind mine
sign sling 2 th revolving opn th box mor its
onlee tendr greetings that cum out 2 th
revolving hem is sheer darklee th upward n
onlee mobile like satin undr foot is wantom
watrs is wavrs th soup nut cannistr triggrs
n was he waiting 4 him all day yu cud ferris
wheel a trembul as s th hand on th maps th
paint tins n me n th waiting ring a triumph
uv day time lighting he herd him say n he
herd what he sd n sigh 4 th victoree danse
n igh 4 th trade wars n thos rite wing
fascists theyr minds evn a redundansee n did
they heer th same thing duz aneewun duz
aneewun know what theyr dewing reelee
nervouslee not knowing evn on site invite
inside partee hide leenin on theyr own
patholojee was it a turbine or was it a fethr
alone at last 2 reelee b worsted th tweed
murdr time untwinning

welcum is bcum i gotta th bcalming b
wethr allowd is dan i was sew tirud
was it th nu pills th lack uv dreem compan
yun i cudint hold up th oceans anee
mor i needid help i wantid 2 shrug but
i was 2 tirud 2 he sd   n th sky it
wasint up 2 me anee mor that feeling
bye bye sky wer we not allowd
2 see th ded anee mor

yu cant alwayze tell
from eeting my frend joy sd

whn i askd what was th food
theyd brout her i know less thn
   nothing i sd i usd 2 know nothing
but that bcame 2 much uv a burdn 4 me
   2 handul yr furthr liberating yrself
she sd yes i hope sew or hope 4
      nothing live within   ium sew
   glad yr heer joy sd   sew am i
i sd n we wer laffing   weud
oftn laffd 2gethr   sins i was
      19 th prson iuv known th
longest in my life   her smile
n her laff undrstanding
      acceptans
theereez going off in my hed
   like fire krakrs   works th
   tieing 2gethr uv sentences
views lines words upholding
   deskribing   ths moment
visiting my frend in her hospital
   room   n thn suddnlee ths nu prson
wheeld in fast n sd 2 me at last
   yuv cum back i told them yu
wud return   n thn th ferriss wheel
   spinning in our heds   claritee
n appresiaysyun uv th sacridness
uv each moment   how was it she askd
      me   it was ok i sd adventurous
iul tell them she sd   wheeling out
   n me n joy smiling mor agen

[O][O][O][O][O][O][O][O][O][O][O][O][O][O][O]
[O][O][O][O][O][O][O][O][O][O][O][O][O][O][O]
[O][O][O][O][O][O][O][O][O][O][O][O][O][O][O][O]
[O][O][O][O][O][O][O][O][O][O][O][O][O][O][O][O]
[o][o][o][o]o[o][o][o][o][o][o][o][o][o][o][o]
[o][o][o][o][o][o][o][o]++[o][o][o][o][o][o][o]
[o][o][o][o][o][o][o]++++++[o][o][o][o][o][o]
[o][o][o][o][o][o]+++++++++++[o][o][o][o]::
::[o][o][o][o]+++++++++++++++++++[o][o][o]
::[o][o][o][o]+++++++++00+++++++++[o][o][o]
::[o][o][o][o]++++++++0000++++++{o}{o}{o}::
::[o][o][o][o]++++++000000+++++[O][O][O]:::
::[O][O][O][O]+++++00000000++++{O}{O}{O}{O}
::{o][o][o][o]+++++000000++++++[o][o][o]:::
:::[o][o][o][o]+++++00000++++++{o][o][o][o]
:::[o][o][o][o]+++++0000+++++++[O][O][O][O]
;;[o][o][o][o]++++++00+++++++++[O][O][O][O]
::{o][o][o][o][o]++++00++++++++++[O][O][O]
::[o][o][o][o][o]++++00+++++++++++[o][o]:::
:::[o][o][o][o][o]+++000+++++++++++[o][o]::
:::[o][o][o][o][o]+++000++++++++++{oooo}::
::[o][o][o][o][o]++++00+++++00++++[oooo}:
::[o][o][o][o][o]++++00++++0000++++[O][O]::
::[o][o][o][o][o]++++00+++000000+++[o][o]::
::[o][o][o][o][o]++++00+++000000+++[O}[O]::
::{o][o][o][o][o]++++00+++000000+++{O}{O}::
::[o][o][o][o][o]++++00+++000000+++{O}{O}::
::{o][o][o][o][o]++++00+++000000+++[o][o]::

great lake erie scape

    th translucent moon
    th translucent star
    th translucent atar
    th translucent rats
    th translucent ar street
    shone thru our bones
     looking up dansing 4
      a bettr world tara sang
       th translusensee uv th
      buzzing ringing thred
      th in4maysyun zones
purvu curtail we walking out 2 th farthest
     uv point pelee swim in th surrounding
   air th infinit translusensee evree
wher th urgent need 2 share
     th translucent harp
      th translucent part uv evreething
    th translucent tarp onlee covring
      th translusensee uv th dark n th
    nite translusensee uv th bats ravens crows
      hawks perch radial wheels salmon pike n
     mackerel cod eagul n sublime swim uv
   th translucent arp t
     th translucent heart
    th translucent art he
   th translucent yu
     th translucent me
   th translucent b n th translucent
     she he shee eezee zee see

was it th translucent atara weeree
uv wundring we or
was it th translucent see
great lake birds cries calling
n th translucent eez uv th amparo
re ruu uuutin zee zephros sha shula
zeeandr komptee zee
lusentya lewsentis lux lucis lucinda xu l
tenya slu sluet ay tens trans ran street
lucite luandra ten spen luce prama
lua lu shula a shuala lu ci si ula
lu see kattul rangr zoft clouds
th sumtimes mewsik uv we

what 2 dew whn sumwun is

trying 2 intrfeer infilitrate with in2 yr
mental life yr processes
dew not yell back
tell them they cant yell at yu   yu
dont go 4 that yu dont take shit from
no wun aneemor n yu ar not a bad
prson

n that they cant hang theyr feers n
angrs
on yu   dont let yrself get caut up
in anee fals merging   hold them
whil they cry in2 yr chest pull out all th
bugs n plugs n ugs n lugs theyr
trying 2 implant in yr vulnrabul
neurons   buffr buffr
fire wall fire wall n separatelee no
mor fals merging yet yu cant 4get abt
them how fritend they ar with th
terribul
unsirtinteez yu worree abt them n
will it evr b how yu thot it was yu
dont know   n yu cry 4

eye went 2 th halo club

2 meet him he nevr showd   i waitid 4
hours i think he was late i had a great
time aneeway next day he phond in
a lengthee xplanaysyun whil i was try
ing 2 undrstand my apartment i didint
undrstand his xplain at all sew i wrote
it down whil he was xplaining it sew i
cud refer 2 it latr
he startid with th time changing n that
was onlee th beginning whn i look at th
lengthee xplain   is th big xplain just
previous 2 th big nap eye still
dont undrstand it or as well
what is IT   th interruptid
fluiditee uv courting rhythms th
ingenious intraksyuns within th bushes
sum moon ovrhed or not we found each
othr n compare n contrast with taking
that in 2 th club life whos ther n who
cudint arriv that nite   wher evreewun
from all ovr town evree walk n style
uv life wud show up n danse n rock
out all th shit n entangulments get
down from evree job place   n th moon
above followd us all heer   keepin th
beet

letting go uv lernd behavyur   meditaysyuns from
gold mountain   reth th abstraksyuns uv langwage
32

th ramshakul witness cud onlee say fingrs n toez mer
engay clapping each hors was n th thundr races thru th
sircutree n th memoreez n th awareness stinging n yet
nevr seen a nite ths dark sumwun attestid n th clovrs
ran bloodee insted uv hung 2 dry 4 th traktor show next
day ahh th injuree uv letting all th mosquitoez in 4 th
nite n that vois agen soaring thru th bords n walls uv th
ancient building was it from th big band era yu know n
th cellophane wrapprs jettisond th salaree n th pink
celeree its just anothr side uv life n thats how g-d made
honkee tonk angels rose briar at th aftrnoon th chorus
uv 4getting n life standards wipe yr shus off n in th
morning th memoree uv being floodid with mosquitoez
sittin on that rock with th perlee sheen n fools gold 2 it
wrapping th polestr ribbon round tow trucks by th
harbour millyun what 2 dew without blame did yu find
th entree form map n th in4maysyun them crayduld up
th stares n me apeering in a dreem 2 him all skeleton
no flesh saying how luckee they wer 2 have each othr
that i didint have that i did think i did 4 a whil but i
reelee didint n i reelee dont n i was sew happee they
did n they phone n wantid 2 know if i was ok i was fine
i sd n thanks sew much 4 calling sew great n unxpektid
2 heer from sew off th line n off th grid n th dolls uv 2
morro we havint met yet ar they alredee inside us sliding
with raymonds embossd essay on loss n self fortitude
whispr th wake ache we can onlee treet th impass with
dot dot who was dot dorotheea uv th evning breezes her
vois running with th nite time winds nestling in th soft
branches singing a sustaining hi note wivering thru th
erlee moon beems spattring n mooring lites thru th

changing rivr n peopuls voices by th great fire in th back
anothr goldn nite her vois th singing whispr uv th galaxee
runs thru us all our skins enthralling threds within threds
strings within strings dissolving reapeering in changing
guises dissolving n reapeering agen nevr holding 4 long
th mewsik uv evreewun continuing evreewher th song
yet straining in2 th tallest sky wher 4evr presumablee no
answr lies

up on gold mountain meditaysyuns on melting
th hard wiring uv lernd behavyur 24

sum nites yu just get th bluez tho evn on gold
mountain no mattr th acheevment uv subtul undr
standings byond narrativ n chunkee cawsalitee
thos ideaz that whn yu ar feeling fine dew reelee
seem retro or yu can know them n th sew manee
othr attendent or not versyuns n yet breeth n dew
things byond theyr push n pull n big reaktiviteez
n thn they can bite yu n th answr i am wher i am
dusint reelee fulfill whn yu c sumwun yu love b
demonstrabulee hot with sum wun els evn tho it
was sd n thot yu wud still get 2gethr sumhow n
now its less n less likelee n i love seeing them b
happee 2gethr runnin off holding hands n cest sa
cest tout dew i leev dew i say aneething can i
schedule 4 ths sketchiness n uv kours we dont
reelee know our futurs but we reelee dont know
th futur it mite happn 4 eithr layrs n threds
trajektoreez n insites desires n planning n thrs
no konklewsyun abt aneething or can thr b
sumtimes n wun prson sd b4 retiring i havint bin
psychikalee sick like yu three have but at thees
late yeers whats diffikult is continualee being alone
not living with aneewun i undrstand i sd but in th
south ium alone n oftn tirud uv it but we dont
know th futur aneething cud happn lookit them
was it reelee how luckee they ar that they found
each othr it cud happn 4 eithr or both uv us n
yet mostlee we ar dewing fine on our own n
lookit th moon half moon 2nite shining thru th
branches uv that eezilee 2–3 hundrid yeer old
tree how resplendent it is being heer with us n

venus sew strong ovr ther n is th bluez why we
think uv leeving gold mountain oftn fine in my
work writing n painting n th attachment problem
atik oftn transcending or 2 retro 2 get in2 th med
itaysyun n th praxis uv kleer thinking working
leeving gold mountain returning 2 th citee sew
much is going on ther we dont think we ar alone
did i cum up heer 4 myself n my souls journee or 2
b with him sumwun whos alredee takn n sd ths or
 that n lovinglee hints uv cum on 4 latr on lovinglee
like whn i was with him b4 ths what oh wud
            happn but it nevr reelee will but i may not
            undrstand also reelee why i was brout heer
            what is th storee gingr n brite orange beeks
            uv 2 ravens partnrs he sd n th deepning blu
            uv th sky n th currents uv th rivr i sat in 2day
            getting probablee 2 much sun oh it was sew
            beautiful n thru th migraine seeing how wun
            prson came 2 call on claim wud b 2 strong but
            it cums 2 mind n th blood vessels in th mind start
            ing 2 inflame n swell with thees love as possesiv
        narrativs n th beautee uv ths place n th wayze uv
        holding peopul iuv nevr reelee lernd like that
        frend sd faraway iuv nevr bin abul 2 hold aneewun
        like   how she came 2 get him from being in th watr
    with me n all thees trajektoreez reduktiv scenarios as
        if its ths or that whn nowun knows tho th that is
            definitlee sumwun 2 sleep with yu love n loves yu
            is that th dreem thru all ths impermanens th moon
            turning whil th erth rotating n mooving say 4ward
    if yu will n th class war n th rich taking evreething
     they can from th rest uv us n th traumas sew

manee uv us found each othr thru n 4 th heeling
    with an othr or with th dreem uv sum othr or
    sleeping in th craydul uv sum starree part uv th
    milkee way we ar in n th shock uv anee hurt
    realizasyun dusint mattr dont bring yr past 2
    gold mountain nor yr futur or anee sidewayze
    conundra n tryin 2 fix anee thing love is not
    possessyun not attachment is it luck
is it whn th moon smiles
  n our tatterd seeming dreems sew
  themselvs
back 2gethr agen without our
    knowing
  n th moon smiles agen
    up on gold mountain

```
{OХOХOХOХOХOХOХOХO]{OХOХOХO]{OХOХOХOХOХOХOХOХO}
[O][O][O][O][O][O][O][O][O][O][O][O][O][O][O][O]
{OХOХOХOХOХOХOХOХOХOХOХOХOХOХOХOХOХOХO}
{OХOХOХOХOХOХOХOХOХOХOХOХOХOХOХOХOХOХO}
{OХOХOХOХOХOХOХO}<*>{OХOХOХOХOХOХO}
{OХOХOХOХOХOХO}<*>{OХOХOХOХOХOХO}
{OХOХOХOХOХOХO}<*><*><*>{OХOХOХOХOХO}
{OХOХOХOХOХOХO}<*><*><*>{OХOХOХOХOХO}
{OХOХOХOХOХO}<*><*><*><*><*>{OХOХOХOХO}
{OХOХOХOХOХO}<*><*><*><*><*>{OХOХOХOХO}
{OХOХOХOХO}<*><*><*><*><*><*><*>{OХOХOХO}
{OХOХOХOХO}<*><*><*><*><*><*><*>{OХOХOХO}
{OХOХOХO}<*><*><*><*><*><*><*><*><*>{OХOХO}
{OХOХOХO}<*><*><*<*><*><*><*><*><*><*>{OХO}
{OХOХO}<*><*><*><*><*><*><*><*><*><*><*><{O}
```

```
{OХO}<*><*><*><*><*><*><*><*><*><*><*><*>{O}
{OХO}<*><*><*><*><*>(=)(=)<*><*><*><*><*>{OХO}
{OХO}<*><*><*><*><*>(=)(=){=}{=}<*><*><*>{OХO}
{OХOХO}<*><*><*>(=)(=)(=)(=)(=)(=)(=)<*><*>{OХO}
{OХOХOХO}<*><*><*>(=)(=)(=)(=)(=)(=)<*><*>{OХO}
{OХOХOХOХO}<*><*><*>(=)(=)(=)(=)<*><*><*{OХO}
{OХOХOХOХOХOХO}<*><*><*>(=))=)<*><*>{OХO}
{OХOХOХOХOХOХOХO}<*><*><*><*><*>{OХO}
{OХOХOХOХOХOХO}<*><*><*><*><*>{OХOХOХO}
{OХOХOХOХOХOХO}<*><*><*>{OХOХOХOХO}
{OХOХOХOХOХOХO}<*><*>{OХOХOХOХOХO}
{OХOХOХOХOХOХOХO}<*>{OХOХOХOХOХO}
{OХOХOХOХOХOХOХOХOХOХOХOХOХOХOХO}
{OХOХOХOХOХOХOХOХOХOХOХOХOХOХOХO}
{OХOХOХOХOХOХOХOХOХOХOХOХOХOХOХO}
{O]{OХOХOХOХOХOХOХOХOХOХOХOХOХO}{OХO}
```

iul nevr 4get that pizza at sunrise

n blak koffee sew thik
with th skarlet blayzing huge n
growing ball clambring ovr
n ovr filling th horizon

that pizza at sunrise on th
pacifik ocean n its spelling life
  breething in us 4 sum decades
manee yeers it stayd with us
th pizza vegetarian sum pine
appul n all our fingrs reeching
  out 2 th brite reddning sun
we wer tall thn n ganglee

  n th brite lite turquoise waves
  alwayze cumming in palms n
    kiyetta freeholeez ths was not
th love that we each wantid but
  maybe it was bettr thn n we
wudint know n ovr th yeers iuv
had pizza in snow fields th tango
uv rice fields

tangereen islands with celeree
treez n it all changing th
companee th time th rind uv
  memoree n th pizza pine
appul chees n our lives

meditaysyun 23 on th stretching materialitee

uv langwage meditaysyuns from gold
mountain n as well as seeing is b leeving tho
not alwayze same with heering n touching th
mountain n th were wolverine n th tempest
raging on th deck whn sailors dscoverd
what they didint want 2 know well sumtimes yu
cant covr evreething osten sighd n sirtinlee lang
wage came from all our fakulteez n ar we
allowd wit whn speeking with ekonomik superiors
can we b equal with them in at leest that way
langwages cum abt thru all our organik being
bcumming changing n progressing 2ward
liquid like watr mooving thru watr or ovr n thru
fresh green fields th portabul sovereigntee uv
each climate lokaysyun lokating n shaping th
length uv each vowell constonant n th entire
theem n variaysyun uv each pronounseeaysyun
its attendent accents how langwage is material like
a kidney th breething livr th vois box lungs th
digestiv systems how th soundings shape n
modify our intensyunaliteez now dew we reelee
know what we ar tho we nevr reelee ar without
bcumming continualee being n empteeing wuns we
all loos our minds rufflee th same time what abt our
hearts we may start 2 reelee begin th adventur uv
evolving evr mor awsum xcelent n we heer th mewsik
uv th treez in manee places as we ar alredee at all times
zond n jonkd n all wayze stiks n stones words reelee
dew have th powr 2 hurt n endangr n wound heel
soothe n instrukt n uplift yes evn without linear arrange
mentz n convenshunul narrativs narrativs what zone n
peel chords sentiments n zeel words ar objekts we
animate thru th air how dew yu say love

its th sailors life

th mercurial mast hed
leeps across th hous n th
revers tuppr weering all th
clothes he cud 2 get out uv a
strange n harmful draft
thos ideas uv angr n reveng will get
yu nowher he sighd make a reel
change insted he sd that
benefits yrself n evreewun

looking 4ward 2
sum chill time soon
just whn a fervid
announsr sout 3
reassurances enuff 2 sleep
by summr was slow 2
cum in ths yeer
n didint last veree long eithr
as beautiful as it was
sumtimez th wind wud take yu
out fine n just leev yu ther 4
th longest time raising nothing
n billys accordion oftn
going all nite n ther was
skuffuling n a tangul or 2 b4 th
nite settuld in n down prtremulo
n it was th strangest dsastr

nowun cud remembr it
in accord with aneewun
els n th dog barking all
nite wer ther reelee no
   parsnips left he was herd 2
sigh undr th left ovr vishyun uv
   th wheetfield trimming n evree
   thing els what have i dunstid
sollo saffro sailor
                    climbs ovr
  oh i remembr th gleem in his
eyez gold it was oui levitating
   tree n th nite starting 2
   settul in coveing th first
street liked or lickd th birds
   flying off 2 zansibar n whrevr
   whatevr wasint that whn we
found each othr n a bodee heevd
  ovr th side o th veree first time we
   glow cudint say aneething abt it he cud
have swam 2 shore we werent that far
   off n th terribul stillness cud have
got 2 him it was 2 yeers ago i tried 2
   write ths down he had sd 2 me
   its th sailors way he sd agen 2 me
      th banalitee uv beautee n evil ar
      marreed 2 each othr theyr baybee
      is us   not us in partikular he sd
   but our specees how our specees

is hard wired thats our challeng
2 rise above whoweer 2 get
outside uv th neuro paradigm
uv our specees 2 step outside uv
th hard iron rung thru us if we can
is th qwestyun n if thers th time
i listend 2 him as th lite fadid n goldn
n turquois nite set in how he talkd
abt our love 4 each othr i had nevr
herd such amayzing talk i had
felt it with him but no wun had
evn sd thees things 2 me as th
ship stilld lulld his arms around
me i was wher i wantid 2 b n no
longr yernd 4 shore life n its
damaging complexiteez
restrikt thos organik lives lines
uv rewards n punishment drawn
thru them all in a dizzeeing dsplay
uv changing rules nowun knows th
sours uv evn that can b aneewher
iud rathr stay heer see thos brite
silkn fish jumping sew hi n th dreem
evreewher witness or sum manee
summrs reveree languores n sew
fine we want love n sex 2 last 4evr
but neithr uv thm duz how th dance
is ther or in ths othr place what
duz last 4evr nothing no mattr
what we dew we lose suffr loss

n thn we want 2 hold
arrange 2 suit or address th
companee n no wun is
bettr companee 4 me thn him
n itul change up proprietal
love is ovr like oil n fossil fuels n
dusint last how hard we ar at
lerning that n th erning each
moment is evr lasting
love can tho n duz oftn 4
manee peopul n nothing can
b evreething n who knows
who reelee knows sept we
love each othr
all uv each
othr
whoevr wherevr no judging
letting go uv all that n th blame
games n reveng n hurting th
jealouseez th rewards n
punishments ovr n ovr agen
n who knows eithr thing or being
truth telling n th loving or yes
evreething that can b glows
soul redolent all th touching bliss
tendr regard
its a sailors way n a
sailors life
n th love th is chilling chilling n
gettin it on th glamour uv th
midnite stairs

from th late aftrnoon now all th nite lites
on n our hearts beeting in time 2 th
watr uv our lives lapping in no des
kripsyun will reelee dew is our lives
        breething bliss avoiding th deep freez
its th way   sew manee wayze n we live
thru sew manee wayze hoisting th ropes
trope mango swabbing th decks heer
        agen ce soir full summr i saw mor
cumming
        in th sky we all can b th venus blessing
th falsetto was thrilling n kind uv wundrful
wher his hands th fire escape n th
        window dressing th moon

        is ths reelee he askd me offring him his
missing hand   gnite he sighd 2 all living
        kreetshurs in th goldn always   its a
        sailors life dreeming th 4evr th
moment is
                        th sailor way

        yes i think i cud live full time with sum
        wun but i dont know if its rite 4 me
        on ths planet   or

i dont know if ths is th rite planet 4 me
        2 dew that yet

arint ther othr places
arint ther othr places is ther
2 b with yu as th way is
a sailors song cud b

cud b maybe iul work on it
n letting go mor each day

our pathwayze lit by diamond
stars

or m m d vid   a a a am or d vi d
davi dada avid avi d
a a am or d vid   a a amor   d vi d
avi d   davi i
a a am or d v i d   m o r   m o   r ad
adda da ada avi via dia dav vadia
diaava via vai dia iad   daaa iiii avid
iav va vavi vid div dav av id a id
did did diva did
did did did did a did a did av did
vadid   did av did va vadid i did i did dav di
avd id dav di dav dav gee dia dav
belovid delovib dilvobe lidvoeb b lo ov
b dav avi iva d d did dad dav vad add id
va
va vaaav va av vaaaaaa did viad
diav vi   veee vaaa avid avid avid dav i
viad vaid   diav idva diva vi vi vaaa avid
div via dav dia iad adi div via via d d
i i i i va va vi vi veee vuuuu uv daa
add via

i remembr th
wun uv th last times
yu wer
crawling ovr my bodee 2
get 2 anothr 2
get 2 her
n th moon was
turning n th u f os pulsing
like th moon pulsing i was
ok we each wer i think
ther waitin 4 yu   n yu wer
climbin ovr her bodee 2
get back 2 me

its a sailors life   soon th road
but 4 now in2 my bodee in2
yu yu in2 me yr bodee yu
n th sun cummin up anothr day
anothr nite n we held each
othr 4 hours until anothr
sun up no time 2 listn 2 bluez
notes in th air time 2 pack n
get kleer n oh i wantid 2 stay
but wher how n thrs no way
n th sun up 4 a whil now
yu walkd me 2 th road i got
on th bus n whn i lookd 2 c u
agen with th love in both our eyez
yu wer gone   its sum kind uv sailors
life ths song

sum prospektiv n present realms uv consciousness

not reelee doubul bookd as i feerd
he came tord me rathr 2 fast stumbuling
    ovr varied sub clawses
in a nut shell what ar yu trying sew
    hard not 2 tell me
i visitid th angel orakul n it was a
reelee beautiful time byond linear
narrativ we wer waiting 2 heer
what they wud say next n wer we at
    all prepard 4 what wud happn
ths summr i promisd myself 2 get 2 th
top uv th roof gardn n look out evn
    wundring what messengr was
cumming in next   sew much on my
    mind wudint thr b 4 yu 2 if all ths
wer going on in yr life how am i gonna
    deel with it wun step at a time yes
yr rite reelee i cud dew that

i wunderd softlee sew as not 2 dsturb th
lightning tremours cud thr b mor 2 ths n i
    knew i wud hope sew
        longs sumwher latr as th moon turns
        ium in his arms anothr nite evn wun
        mor time

north amerika is way 2 much

espousing th valus uv xtreem
competishyun rivalree btween
individuals is praisd   its 2
much rival me ths ths decay
 ing planet we ar destroy
 ing 2 fuel our contests evn th
giraffes ar leeving

8% uv canadians own ovr
 60% uv evreething in
 canada   1% uv evreewun
in th yewnitid states own
 84% uv evreething ther
  whats th point

uv hungr n homeless peopul
hanging ovr grates on sidewalks
 in th freezing kold   n getting
 pneumonia   in our hostile
  streets

whats th point

its anothr hiway

what is th soul
      but that we dreem it
what is th soul
      but that we live it
i held yu in my arms n hands
thn sumthing moovd
n i held th air in my hands
  both ar wundrful
  yu ar bettr
anothr unreel comparison

  n th will uv th wind
oftn desiding manee uv
  th changes nothing evr
pans out 4 long th glint uv
  th gold in th passing lite
n i begin 2 accept not onlee dew
  i belong with th wind but i live in
th words n images thats wher
what n who lives in my heart

  just coz i like yu bettr
   thn air dusint meen yul
stay go ovr it agen air
  dusint stay it is n th fools gold
shines as well n th hot sun uv th
life n th rivrs song moovs within me
  evn as i find a quiet place by th rivr

45

in th north 4 my dottrs ashes n thos
uv her son i clambr down on th
rocks thr is no wind i mix theyr
ashes 2gethr n emptee th bag ovr
th watr ther is no wind n thn th wind
cums up fast n thrs ashes ovr me n th
rocks most uv th ashes went in2 th
watr i brush th ashes off my t shirt
in2 th watr from my bodee saying
gud bye agen we ar all part uv each
othrs bodee i tell them i will alwayze
love them i was honourd 2 have
wundrful brillyant timez with them n i
thankd them n my eyez filling up got
in2 sum chanting th hunee chant
i usd 2 dew all th ringing n amayzing
love we shard ashes ovr me thers
always sum slap stik n yu nevr know
tho yu can think yu will   how th wind
will go
evn if yu belong 2 it

what is th soul
that we dreem it
what is th soul
that we live it

th singing uv spirits n spiritual th
chattring horses ovr that rivr ther n th

racoon lookout chorus uv voices ovr th
sparkling changing rivr   soothes us sew
       fine as nothing els can   love is as loves
bereft sooth th sayer on mountain tops
n basement zero n aneewher inbtween
     th trubul is in th attachment th fire
          finds us n whethr it matches n 4
how long th summr inside th moment
       each moment a galaxee we live in
thru its a beautiful galaxee n find it
       sumwher els whn it subsides cant yu

       wher can th wanderer stay
     thers less heer thn ther but th naytur is
     beautiful

       what is th soul
               that we dreem it
     what is th soul that we live it
          n love   all th care it asks 4 n th
benefits n th ikon taybuls
       n giraffe glass wear

47

```
[*X*X*X*X*X*X*X*X*X*X*X*X*X*X*X*X*X*X*X*}
{*X*X*X*X*X*X*X*X*X*X*X*X*X*X*X*X*X*X*X*}
{*X*X*X*X*X*X*X*X*X*X*X*X*X*X*X*X*X*X*X*}
{OXOXOXOXOXOXOXOXOXOXOXOXOXOXOX:O}
[<O>X<O>X<O>X<O>X<O>X<O>X<O>X<O:
{<O>X<O>X<O>X<O>X<O>X<O>X<O>X<O:
{<O>X<O>X<O>X<O>X<O>X<O>X<O>X<O:
{<O>X<O>X<O>X<O>X<O>X<O>X<O>X<O:
{IXIXIXIXIXIXIXIXIXIXIXIXIXIXIXIXIXI}:
{IXIXIXIXIXI}XIXIXIXIXIXIXIXIXIXIXI};
{IXIX{I}[I][I][I][I][I][I][I]X[I][I][I][I][I][I][I][I][I][I][I]::
{IXIXIXIXIXIXIXI}XXX{IXIXIXIXIXIXIXI}
{IXIXIXIXIXIXIXI}XXXXXX{IXIXIXIXIXIXI}
{IXIXIXIXIXIXI}XXXXXXXXX{IXIXIXIXIXIXI}
{IXIXIXIXIXI}XXXXXXXXXXXX{IXIXIXIXIXI}
{IXIXIXIXI}XXXXXXXXXXXXXXX{IXIXIXIXI}
{IXIXIXI}XXXXXXXXXXXXXXXXXXX{IXIXIXI}
{IXIXI}XXXXXXXXXXXXXXXXXXXXXX{IXIXI}
{IXI}XXXXXXXXXXXXXXXXXXXXXXXXX{IXI}
{I}XXXXXXXXXXXXXXXXXXXXXXXXXXXX{I}
{I}XXXXXXXXXXXXXOXXXXXXXXXXXXXX{I}
{IXI}XXXXXXXXXXXOOXXXXXXXXXXXXX{IXI}
{IXIXI}XXXXXXXXOOOOOXXXXXXXXX{IXIXI}
{IXIXIXI}XXXXXOOOOOOOOXXXXX{IXIXI}:
{IXIXIXIXI}XXXXOOOOOOOOOXXXXX{IXIXI}
{IXIXIXIXIXIXI}OOOOOOOOOOOXXXX{IXIXI}::
{IXIXIXIXIXIXI}XXXXXOOOOOXXXXX{IXIXI}
{IXIXIXIXIXIXIXIXIXI}OOOOXXXXX{XIXIXIX}:
{XIXIXIXIXIXIXIXIXIXIXIXIXIXIXIXIXIX}:
{XIXIXIXIXIXIXIXIXIXIXIXIXIXIXIXIXIX}:
```

```
{<:>}{<:>}{<:>}{<:>}{<:>}{<:>}{<:>}{<:>}{<:>}{<:>}{<:0>}
{<:>}{<:>}{<:>}{<:>}{<:>}{<:>}{<:>}{<:>}{<:>}{<:>}{<:0>}
{<:>}{<:>}{<:>}{<:>}{<:>}0000{<:>}{<:>{<:>}{<:>}{<:0:>}
{<:>}{<:>}{<:>}{<:>}0000000000000{<:>}{<:>}{<:>}{<:0>}
{<:>}{<:>}{<:>}{<:>}00000000000000{<:>}{<:>}{<:>}{<:>}
{<:>}{<:>}{<:>}00000000000000000000000{<:>}{<:>}{<:>}
{<:>}{<:>}0000000000000000000000000000{<:>}{<:>}
{<:>}{<:>}0000000000000000000000000000{<:>}{<:>}
{<:>}{<:>}{<:>}000000000000000000000{<:>}{<:>}{<:>}
{<:>}{<:>}{<:>}0000000000000000000{<:>}{<:>}{<:>}
{<:>}{<:>}{<:>}{<:>}00000000000000{<:>}{<:>}{<:>}{<:>}
{<:>}{<:>}{<:>}{<:>}00000000000000{<:>}{<:>}{<:>}{<:>}
{<:>}{<:>}{<:>}{<:>}00000000000000{<:>}{<:>}{<:>}{<:>}
[<:>}{<:>}{<:>}{<:>}00000000000000{<:>}{<:>}{<:>}{<:>}
{<:>}{<:>}{<:>}00000000000000000000{<:>}{<:>}{<:>}
{<:>}{<:>}{<:>}00000000000000000000{<:>}{<:>}{<:>}
{<:>}{<:>}{<:>}00000000000000000000{<:>}{<:>}{<:>}
{<:>}{<:>}{<:>}00000000000000000000{<:>}{<:>}{<:>}
{<:>}{<:>}{<:>}00000000000000000000{<:>}{<:>}{<:>}
{<:>}{<:>}{<:>}00000000000000000000{<:>}{<:>}{<:>}
{<:>}{<:>}{<:>}000000000{I}0000000000{<:>}{<:>}{<:>}
{<:>}{<:>}{<:>}00000000{I}{I}000000000{<:>}{<:>}{<:>}
{<:>}{<:>}{<:>}0000000{I}{I}{I}00000000{<:>}{<:>}{<:::>}
{<:>}{<:>}{<:>}{<:>}000{I}{I}{I}{I}000{<:>}{<:>}{<:>}{<:>}
{<:>}{<:>}{<:>}{<:>}00{I}{I}{I}{I}{I}{I}{<:>}{<:>}{<:>}{<:>}
{<:>}{<:>}{<:>}{<:>}{<:>}{I}{I}{I}{I}{<:>}{<:>}{<:>}{<:>}{<:>}
{<:>}{<:>}{<:>}{<:>}{<:>}{<:>}{<00>}{<:>}{<:>}{<:>}{<:>}{<:>}
{<:>}{<:>}{<:>}{<:>}{<:>}{<:>}{>00<}{<:>}{<:>}{<:>}{<:>}{<:>}
```

who   wud

want 2 live   yu cant catch
in a hauntid   evreething ar yu
hous with   living in that beautiful
ghosts   vallee i remembr loamee
i alredee why wud i   n th sun n th
 melodee uv
have   ocean streem neerby
memoreez   i hope its all gud with yu
ar yu awake   heer whn nite settuls its
ar yu awake   veet all ovr us oranges thn
                       deep blu thn black

no moon
 walkin thru a why wud i   from heer n th
                        sounds uv th
4est uv cedar   endless traffik n th lake air
 oak spruce   in our nostrils   th traffik sounds
 pine n fir   like an ocean ths workshop needs
mor leesyur space
 dew yu live why wud yu what happend next
 onlee in yr   n how it was
mind   wher els who wud   was it ok did it
   pleez yu wher els now that yuv bin 4givn moan
 can yu grab love whil yu can ar yu th listnr plan
    a is missing plan b is prettee
 sketchee plan c is yu i can hardlee
   heer yu th drilling outside but what yu ar
 saying sounds reelee interesting th melodee
 uv have ar yu still in treetment like me th opn
   ray glow uv yr mind   is it evr what yu think it is
 that opning is it seald   i herd yu whispr

gloria

th treez ar rising in th august rain
a veil uv cloud mercurial mist n vapor
hanging ovr th erth th greens n th
oranges n browns all look mor sew

gloria yr lettr is weird 4 me abt
don n th relativs who was lax n
who was mor dutiful
              i dont know

    cud it b ther ar manee wayze not
  onlee wun way 2 judg each othr
    n is ther th time 2 judg

          ium letting go uv thees concerns
           yu n me n don n th othrs
              parteeing laffing 2gethr
           loving each othr ths is what i
           want 2 recall now 2 help me
           in th present on my way

     tho yeers latr i undrstand mor
   uv what yu wer saying n thrs
     evn less i can dew abt it now
   tho sumimes i wish i cud tho
    not always nothing is its our
intro 2 th theem uv dsapeering
narrativs non binaree non universal
   a fansee from b4 tho that did happn but
its a veree prsonal realm that cant b stoppd
or rewrittn words in watr ovr th falls

why i write

                                          7 hands lapping 7
                    gettin th nus out   ands apping
           as us poets have alwayze dun
           whats goin on at court th govrn
           ment th secret corporate xploitrs
           th senate th who th breth in th
                    lettrs love   being
           speeking out against injustis
           n th melodeez that cum in2 wun
thru wuns ear th colours n shapes uv
           th words lettrs thru wuns brain
           phrases paradigms that as if on

           theyr own cum in2 me yu heer th
           mewsik uv th awning in th summr
           breez   th humiditee
              resting 4 a moment   nu verbal
           approximaysyuns n all th ocean deep
              phrases
                    images   th 4est inside th mango
           birds n th orange streekd antlrs
                    uv th tortois flyrs livrs he

                    mooving thru th nouns n
                    verbs th green darkness
                    n suddn purpul lite

                    if i can write down as
                    they usd 2 say i arm my
                    self un arm myself
                    relees me
                    from me agen
                    from me un fettr

my self n th lettrs un fret myself
get th frets in places 4 th
tonaliteez traces n tropes
teez th laces find a shu show shape
wher th self is was can b relees th
we from me tellin storeez uv th me
th yu 2 say sing sorrow xpress n b
get it out me myself n i i yu
write n tellin storeez uv th we   how
we ar me   n how we th me how
me ar we   n how we th we   th breth
in th lettr n how me th we n how
we th we   th evreething
sentences
wher is th me th we
n th beautee uv th lettrs themselvs th
word words ords w kay danse
phrase syntax syntaxes me n aces

we   telling tilling telling sew
manee phases   hap phosphorescent
in th still glowing moonlite phrases
trilling   th runes fell haphazardlee

talling tulling tolling spaces
n timez folding in out our
changes chances cognitiv dee
mensyunal shiftings continua zee
cogtinua we lookin out at th rivr
sing

sharpning th listning pallette 4   substans
storee how we surviv our disapointments fan
taseez   saying th   bridges btween lettr
wods feeling th words woods 4 n meditating no
storee being what being n
approach 2   noun th pickshur verb telling a thousand
words in partikular
2nd hand words 3rd 4th hand words
saying fifth i want 2 live with yu 4evr
sighing making glad   emblems
uv th
ideas feelings adverb
seventh fulfilling am i
making a thousand pickshurs why i
write
2 describe animate bring 2 life as
they usd 2 say with all its
complexiteez n what isint storee is
bcumming th lafftr pain th allowing
say sing sun ound th yu objektiv
realist ar   undeskribing sew
yu psychiatrik subjektivist e
pistemolo whats th trewth
jee who did what 2 whom
how th
we was destroyd was it evr
ther   sumtimes yes
sumtimes no sew
keep sewing it knowing it
evn knarlee th yarn n th darning

n re build agen organik spiritualist

sew manee views th almost
                                almond

            rhapsodik
        romanticisms we oftn feel
            sew manee mareen tautolojeez
            n erthling sumtimes loosness
            whn whr th brain n its wirings
        prmit we have th paprs 4 n how
            that happend
        n what that versyun did duz 2 me
        n we   th kaleidoscope in june
            th w n th m ar up inside each othr
                endless
            lee all told getting
    th suppliez in 2 show
    n tell nu writing nu painting
    nu free
            doms insites standing undr
    th describing n undescribing
        storeez
            uv
    n un storeez   oreez uv me n we
        eez or was th door a jar is
        a bell a ringing
    th taybul a plate howevr
    temporaree   th piano was on sturdee
        mars   a lavendr carpet uv gasoleen
                ro zee   th wind a no

55

nonsens barrell uv floating fire
appuls getting our storeez out whil
   th air is n cud sing th lettrs sew
taktile a needid

                     sens 2 relees th
taktilitee uv th shaping
                     endorphins
                     th lettrs
                          sew skulpturd
     fluid n elektrik

                     within time like
talking with close

                     frends reeding a
     pome by sum wun

                          whil or writing
     wun thers time

                          our hearts touch
     each othr whil

                     thers still time
n breth evn tho us humans ar th
     worst specees on erth

     words have effekts on our
heering on our dna words yelld at us sd
soothinglee softlee 2 us takn in
     how we deskribe ourselvs 2
     our selvs our self valu
                     our memoreez
     chromosomes protein
phernomes th smells we give out
          evn our dna

n lernd behavyurs
                    our evreething
langwage is th see
                    we swim in th

bath we take dailee   naratolojee
c all th doors n windos burping
   banging burning   tres itching with th
chemical circutree we sumtimez
   drown in th brain its raining
   narrativs how we intrpret is how
we akt   sorting out th elipses   th pan
   tried   pouteen   in th inkreesing
   evreething influens d kon
                    strukting sew
   much loosn th wiring
      sum sew we have sum chances
   at happeeness   accepting diffrences
thats wher that starts sew we can
                    bingo bridg
n who works 4 who n how much
   a well is a deep
         image pome   th desert in yr gud eye
same as th opnings at th bottom uv
pyramid lake nevada   that go all th
                    way   they wud say
      2 china   n we still ate desserts thn
ther ar sew manee approaches 2
                    speeking

speeking   th eye is speeking th
    weev is th eye is speeking
        speeking
    th eagul talks   n how we talk
        ar parts
    uv our evolving n how we can
e volv wher wud we b sans tropay our jest
    yurs gestalts points places modes in
 her his it theyr mimetika places emosh hierarkikul
    ekonomonik ikons klass n gendr moteefs sum
    countreez in europe n austin n medicine hat
      have tiny homes 4 homeless peopul how we
      can evol 4 evn 2 have
      no enemeez in th kastul th stupa
        th plain   th vinyards n th seeming
      endless staircases   we ar un stedee
    n disapeering same with evreething
    apeering n disapeer all th markings
        th winds
      have gone now we ar porous not solid as
    much as we think we ar can we evolv beyond
      proprietal love frozn in time obdurate in
          space 2 what end goal bcumming statelee n
      melting let up all th spinning spelling floating
          paradimes turning on inside th communitee
            is evreewun lyrik sound vizual politikul
              narrativ non narativ fuseyun
    n th tornado whers th storee now oww
  lightning flashes that blind th will
leeving 400 houses demolishd n

    unusualee no deths sew far

    in its wake

anshula rhapsodee

❤ also uv kours th effekts uv seeming rejeksyun on peopul ❤

random imp dimena sha impedimenta ÷ ÷ ÷ ar thees voices
in th nite howling winds trilemantaysyuna branches uv dreems
falling crash clump on th ramshakul deck itself abt redee 2 collaps
who did what first was on th speed rink getting in fast tornado sew
cumming voices weul have yr room redee all nite we saw outdoor
chairs flying in th wind fiers branches splitting from 2 hundrid yeer
old treez n he was repeeting 2 me ☐ i dont let aneewun stay in
my bed long that way they cant leev if they wer nevr ther yes i think
i undrstand i sd sighing sew it seemd th winds cud heer n th glass
shook sum mor almost breking n th thundr huge thundring rocks in
th sky n a lightning strike as tall as 3 worlds did a lift up 2 th top uv
ths milkee way galaxee its a hedg insurans he went on cumming tord
me ❤☐☐÷÷♟❤✔ dew yu undrstand he sd ❤♫÷☐♟✔
i think sew i mouthd th words sew softlee ❤ a huge branch flying in
a left opn window grayzing my skin ☐☐☐☐☐ dont rub my eyez
let it in ☐☐☐☐☐☐☐☐☐☐☐☐☐☐☐☐☐☐☐☐☐☐☐☐ ♟

its a hedge against dspair he addid ÷ ✔ ÷ sews ths i hope i addid

**fontinbleu who els wrote abt
n th marigolds
apeering at th**

impassyund bliss   yu cud heer
them n th nu group th hypothetikuls
ovr th long lagoon sew dreemee n
e ll an lan gu ours ours 2 lang uish
th tendrils trembling th slide guitar
sounding sew rich ovr th watr shed
n tigr lilleez n skorchd n rustid freightrs
alex sd he cudint see goin ovr 2 th bliss
wunderd wud all our dreems cum trew
ther 2 make th effort   wud that evr
happn now
why dew yu think
it cant happn i askd it reelee cud is
ther sew much societal panik bcoz
evreewun realizes nowun is going 2
make it get caut up with th costs th
rich ar reelee outwitting evreewun n
theyr big feet ar resting firmlee on all
our heds nevr mind not 2 worree thats
not evreething   sumtimes its anothr
poor prsons feet on our heds   ar yu thn
sew dispiritid   prhaps th magik flying
away   sew far n hi flying with them   2
places yuv
nevr bin isint that what we all want   2 go
yes 2 go 2 places wev nevr been   mind
th opnings   at heart sew yes madiks

tax reform   tax reform tax reform   tax
    reform   that will help 2 inkrees taxes
on rich peopul n rich corporaysyuns
  that will strengthn th countreez tresuree
n make homes 4 th homeless n strengthn
    medicare thats what will help
  n moovs tord guaranteed minimum
incums in spite uv th yew s n our own
  rich ruling class art transcends politiks n is
a place uv refuge in spite uv th evangelikul
    fundamentalists who have no bizness in
    politiks separate church n state
      thats what will help
    thats what will help   h e l p

alex went off 2 see fountinbleu they tossd
  a ball 2gethr sd shit life is hard n strange
sum times we get 2 make sum reel beautee
  regardless 4 a bit alwayze in debt   onlee
sumtimes au courrant thn sumthing changes
  it changes   gets bettr   4 a whil fountinbleu
sd iuv got sum time b4 th gig 2nite cum heer
  alex   in my arms   ths is it cest sa   what we
cum from n is allowd wev gone
  that far   dreeming in th sponjee shade
    lets take it   yeh alex sighd

  dreem uv a stedee gig   gud labour practises in
    akademia   arts institusyuns not 4 profits a
    stedee man   ther wer thos not 2 stedee tho what
      is all th trewisms abt dog eet dog   n strange
kontrakts love can still sumtimes brek thru if
  sumthings a bummr ther dont go aneemor dew
with what yu can with what can b positiv try anothr
    approach   find a place 4 a galleree 2019
    th rents

n still have sum cucumbr sandwiches n
no mattr   love is th greatest gift
fontinbleu   on th magik swing
fontinbleu   reeding a great nu book
fontin bleu being loving with a frend
fontinbleu dewing th dishes
fontinbleu holding his migrains hed
undr th kold watr tap
fontinbleu   chillin 2 start agen
fontinbleu
fontinbleu
fontinbleu
at last in love
n takes th epik journee
fontinbleu feels a sens
uv wondr   fontinbleu
fontinbleu
fontinbleu
fontinbleu
happee at last

n thn th avalanche came n they
wer all bureed in th littul town uv
nothing is missing   n they all
dug themselvs out   shivring n
shakin n wundrin is it evr
reelee that we know th futur n
how interruptid our plans
can bcum

meditaysyuns from gold mountain 11

with life yu nevr know letting go continuing
unseeting th tyrannee uv lernd behavyurs finding
trew rivr by th love   n all along i thot yu wer
at a rib fest in aurora whats th big idea content
n how binaree contentshus nusworthee condiment
ten trembling condos in yu cant have three in a
canoe its sew trew we didint get 2 th trestul or
coniverous if th stewarding uv th paddling
conassenting con descends th eezee 2 deel
mesurs n a wheetfield floating zyglo spinning
finding wunselvs aftr th changing constonant
convoy con way knok on whosewevr retolding
th telling tells continualee constant i can b 4 mor
thn a whil n i like it a constant witness 2 sew yr
evr by yrself figs wer our stipulatid that altrnativ
r constant n constanteen wer theyr alan beware
n data told nevr setting referens points bedpontin
g wasint it th docking plan had gobsmacking
amuck tendrils didint know what 2 ponrify or
ncoherens n coherent inchoate coheer ho
aha i sd 2 th cracking up from th ground less
thn a meter away from me remem bring my
unkul who was elektrokutid by lightning
ahaa i yelld out thinkin 2 rush in n made a reel
impakt is th binaree naytur uv langwage an add
on abstraksyuns 4mind control ar we lost thn
endlesslee in up n down in n out acceptid
rejektid all thees opposits create dilemas uv
posihyuning in rite wrong th prson stuk in th
binareee grammar infinitlee conjuring our
selvs in boxes uv our own making sigh can
aneewun reelee get in par xample ium pro
jekting on2 yr projeksyuns touch yu me
langwage making fluid our conneksyuns

also imprisoning th prson moov th i n is sew
diffrent from th materialitee uv langwage th
uttrances cummin from all th sounds n
pickshurs sprouting spouting from our being
s as in talk therapee how we frame in lang
wanga how we prseev ewhat duz what n how
patterns brain based n lernd all th
spekulativ film noir realism uv our lives
n who deekonstrukt th ovrlays n breeth in th
artikuls th ingredients th bill 4 inkreesd e
qualitee was sidesteppd agen inkoheerans
lapping on th shores uv such poisond inten
syunaliteez who wants less evn espeshulee
at th top tackee is as tackee duz th arktik pix
qween settul in th niagaran laffs evreewun
get yr laffs heer j font languishd longr thn
thot wud he m cudint dscern now at all th
time uv th dill n th time uv th silk dash ref
erensing th immaterialitee uv langwage by th
jnk li th 40,000 yeer old k crying 4 th food
wud we sallee reserv remembr appoint
ments tailor th phras n th seem sew lining
n th crueltee uv parametrs ibnfskk long twe
est btweekr bsilkmmmm ium marshall n mar
sh mallows n hung out me n th keepr oh
man did yu stay out all day waitin on what
maybe it wud b next time th sailors way is
int cumming up heer robert inn szwhat ar yu
dewing he walks in2 my apartment life is in
th wheel keeps on turning n sew on did yu
think that was 2 seveer whatevr or ar yu
weering th stars ar yu starting 2 have likes

will it serv yu yet evreewun is sumwher hour glass
net its a beautiful galaxee n neptune in retrograde
veree unusual its usualee mercuree but th huge
floppee fish tails n how 2 get ths book 2 wch prin
tr duplikator sales n servis is it abt who wants us
n who we want n how 2 combo th went grade see
hors in th brain marros th lifting radius tantamount
2 th beech can we go 4 th day i reelee want 2 feel
yu in my mouth agen isint it wundrful we ar givn ths
time 4 love ths time in our lives yes i sd noting dia
log 2 remembr i wud next nevr use but its awsum 2
remembr he sd it wud i alwayze see th sun in his
beem th bells rang 4 twelv 12 brillyant bells rang
n he was feeling audaysyund enuff 2 ask how did
th meeting go th erth still turning thers a kreetshur
in th wall n sumwuns returning sleep walking that
nite in june was it i tried 2 get out n i cud feel th
thin veil btween ths world th materialitee uv lang
wage th wage uv lang th tongue uv langwage
that it came from th thorax vois box lungs n f f f
feelings shaping ovr millenia rudimentatreek miasma
th membrane tretchr stone teechr adamant nettie
touching th boiling plate yelping 4 joy that she re
kovring wad n jeremee jonathab februaree th time
running out n in a dangling with mesures n
unsirtintee how leeksward th undire surlee way
yu cud heer th clapping from inside th mountain
harrange can yu touch th changing calibrate th
fluid moment gaining on each othr like hungree
hyeenas mooving in 4 th kill but what did yu reelee
think he askd me touching my leg mor firmlee
ths time

icarus was taking 5 dayze off 2
go 2 th sun   a re writing

he didint know why he just knew
he needid th time off   2 manee appointments
can make yu sick whn yu cud b xclent n happee
left him with not enuff time 2 develop his wings
n whoevr th time th sweet preshyus time not 2
waste it   sew heud bettr fly   sew he built
thees huge wax wings they workd well
close 2 th ground
n evn a littul highr whn he was caut
up in an unnamed wind vortex that tuk him
off evn highr
at first
ar we alwayze going up
he was happee with ths
development he was
mooving sew fast
in th at mos pheer
thn th stratospheer
thn he bcame 2 b was in
a mooving byond mooving
byond time n space 2
byond byond all what
our grammar dusint eezilee
say
til a lovr missd him sew
much n calld him n he
refound joy in creaysyun
with a frend making sound poetree
on th cell n he yelld out i can live
as they made sounds 2gethr
ium not dscouragd byond bringing

myself back in i can still reed enuff
uv my own hand writing on th wall
n whos wall is it aneeway   n he landid
in a field uv ice brrrr
ths was indeed a mirakul 4 landing
ther koold his almost starting 2 melt
wings he had bin ther close 2 his
wings bursting
in2 flames
sew he waftid
2 erth n fell in2
th arms uv his lovr
n his frends   home agen
thanks 2 th byond n
thanks 2 th secret handshake
that meets th eye iul take
it on that wun give me 5
n th dayze uv milk shakes n
sardeens no n lafftr n shared
undrstandings ther was
nothing like it as they usd 2
say ths koffee is inkredibul
lets put th wings away 4

a whil ium glad 2 b back n 4
ward as well walking who evr
walkd that way in2 my own
life heer   without wings n i
hope
evreething   turns out ok 4
all uv us

writtn 4 wes rickert
n kathleen reichelt

i was alredee dementid

return(ing) at dusk with sum shadows
    in theyr mind th compleetlee honest
prson found no key undr th side door mat
n th alredee present doubts magnified
in theyr sens uv events n betrayals
    beggd 4 a whol reset if possibul
asap

    thn a loud baritone vois belting
evreething in moderaysyun deep in2 th
  yawning gulping abyss ths is th journee
   uv a life time or is it th vois continued
  thn anothr sound ths wun mite have a bodee
attachd 2 it mite

throttuling th side door on th othr side uv
ths maybe hauntid hous figurs passing by
diaphanous n clumsy our compleetlee
 honest prson sighd ths is asking 4 troubul
ium getting outta heer i dont need 2 b th

centr uv aneething or figur aneething
out ths tresur is indeed being guardid by
  demons n annoying game playrs or
ar they is a compleet thot possibul in
  langwage

in part inspird by th first word uv BIG TOWN
awsum visual konkreet work by hart broudy

th first meditaysyun from gold mountain
with life yu nevr know releesing ourselvs

from sum lernd behavyur can we n sorting out wch
is gud 4 us n wch isint   like they dew in romantik
 mooveez find th erotik balans btween rousseau we
ar born knowing nothing n plato thinking we ar born
 knowing evreething whn th dopomin n serotonin
ar in such a complementaree living moment with
 each othr th elan vital evn if sum awsum doktors
 say thos terms ar metaphors 2 othrs theyr chemikal
fluiditeez in tandem n in c qwensing balansing ar
reel n sew full uv wundrs rewarding each breth
with being n bcumming   reelee ther wher ther
is evn wher ther is no wher

n didint he offr his rekalibraysyuns or was it th boiling
ovr as what did yu think turning 2 th ubiquitous calum
neez a simpul yes or know will undue sunset rule if yu
can greed th likelee sew much th bettr or seed th likes
 th lilee fluttrs n fan dan sing in riotous th winds wud it
b a carrot that wud tame whoevr as in ths moment no
men who wud he take him or them whirling th nutmeg n
not it sorro well thr was sorro plenteous uv it n th rivr
was rising agen n th filigree tonsils cud onlee tissu b
spred sprinkuld toe vaulting thr must b sumwun els
bside th monstrous talcum how lite on her feet she
was aneeway it was strange links posishyund n ran
dom designd   in sum dsallignd mor dsshellvelment no
mattr 2 her or him th how th jaundisd tigr wept at th
 opning was going in it was a cave deepr thn anee
imagining n nevr th less tord felisitous wer th taste
buds uv sweet lafftr th trail mix n avacado he almost
let go uv him hanging from th 7 floor th but he didint
yet it was if thr wer nothing left btween them from

his intrest or evreething was but him n he was
rising above content he needid 2 stay longr 2 develop
an exit otra hedee as th fur deposits in th grain silos
dstrikts wer freqwentlee punkshuatid with larva n
molekular peerlee starrd zylophones it wasint eezee 2
dry all th towells espeshulee in ths rainee wethr

n relees uv lernd bhayuur from continuing meditaysyun
gud diet xercising deekonstruking narrartiv modules
that ar striktness on th hampr line odilaysyuns on th
frakshurd n langethred zenus or trankward how similset
th markward talee resiprositee is it wun o wun or wun
sumwherward summree oh feel that breez n th hi hills
winthin naytur oh thees berreez theyr th best saying no
saying yes takes yu out uv th hi chair yu dont want 2
b in all yr life waaa bo hoo ths is not what i want en
joy th changing la ronde retelling sew manee versyuns
n whn yu want 2 leev th deck n go in 4 a whil n if they
want yu 2 stay as long as yu can bizness n th road
love n th road we ar bcumming acrobats on th hi wire
balansing all th ths n that yu cud b all day wringing out
th tempoareeness uv th ufos n th gladiator hand drawn
summr n wintr scenes enamel applikay oh thers a call
4 yu put th corn in first ok th watrs boiling now sew
yu dont need langwage onlee as representaysyun
same as yu dont need 2 paint onlee background n 4
ground all space is all space   langwage is not onlee
how 2 dew things its also a sours uv reverens n
play play well play fairlee well gertrude stein sd

n eddee n th bruisrs cumming up from th running
they wer dewing on th rivr i go inside hopeing th
eldr who i respekt n have a lot uv feeling 4 wunt let
them in his place but he duz hes hospitabul n th
turning uv th wheel is in full swing

i lovd thos dayze

on th farm in saskatchewan
didint yu that was a
lovlee phase

remembr th autumn desire ther
remembr th crows n th snow
remembr what yu calld me
what happns with time
thers onlee each moment

remembr our jackits
          sparkling in th glacier heet

now we ar heer thers no holes
in our souls is that wher we fell
thru th ice breking on th lake

micro organisms ar brillyant
big planets ar dens they perform
xcellent surgeree thos micro
organisms hilarious n deeplee
disturbing n they ar capabul uv
horrifik intimasee

aftr that we wer interruptid by a
call from space n we cannot
remembr thanks 2 th astro

logikal servis charges systems
n stratajeez an asterik in innr
space

evn th interrupsyuns wer
              interruptid

i lovd thos dayze was writtn with
miles benton chad juriansz n julio

i was secretlee in th

childrns wing uv th hospital
th stitchd up wound in my
leg had 2 b opend as it had
bcum infektid 2 th bone
had it bin sewn up 2 soon
by th doktor who did illegal
aborsyuns 4 us n our frends

i wasint getting pain med
akaysyun as thr cud b no
record uv me being ther th
pain was xkrushiating

my partnr thn she came in
ium just heer 2 use th bathroom
she sd   she came out n sd
2 me why ar yu heer why ar
yu always in hospitals

bcoz yu threw a plate at me
that cut thru 2 th bone n ium
secretlee heer til it heels no
meds ar happning yu threw a

plate at me   thats no xcuse
she sd almost yelling n leeving
looking mor beautiful thn evr

we had had sew manee beautiful
adventurs 2gethr flying ovr pyramid

lake in nevada lifting off from th caves
ther far ovr wher thrs a hole in th
lake th peopul ther sd goez all th way 2
china

they reelee spoke that way thn n
now evree countree is as close as
all our undrweer

n we hope that helps they sd it wud

meditaysyun 30 from gold

mountain dspelling n dsolving hard wiring uv lernd
behavyur remembr its onlee mimikd n lernd not essen
shul whatevr if aneething can b essesnhul that meens
sew thrs all wayze fluiditee thr is no wun langwage
centr langwage centrs ar all ovr th bodee it can b dun
not maybe evreewun at th same time wish beleef what
is it ther is no end its always th beginning memoreez
ar evreewher in on

     our bodeez goldn wishing singing in evree cell
tissu n skin lookit that strange lynx go running
   thru th opning in th 4est ovr ther c th air moov

y th gentul rain full uv doves fall on us
      darkning trembling kreetshurs
              heer gun
     shots in th lowr vallee still
            sum dstans
    away run go let go uv our
feers run 2
     th sun at th top uv gold
mountain go
   theyul nevr kno
    wher we go th realm wher
  ther is no wher
  espeshulee 2
zeno n mercuree freezing th fire
   just a few hektares
    away go

n th goldn lite ths morning
how it remindid me uv our time
on erth didint it yu

n did i evr tell yu
abt th time i was walking
with that prson along th skraggelee
see shell cliff edg see shore n th waves
thundring n roaring in sumtimes seem
ing 2 deliberatelee hit th ground rocks
all th frantik wet in th air n th waves
hugelee rising n falling n drenchd in
nostalgia we wer down from th
cliff soaking wet almost warm
in th erlee fall rain getting cut on
th rocks a bit we came upon
a see cave n went in
2 what seemd like a sereez uv
rooms th first room we wer in was long n less
wide walls mauv emerald smooth n shinee
n giving off a soothing lite n th sound
from th c oftn piersing as if 2 say wake n yet we
wer sew sleepee in th large emerald room with silvr
taybuls n yet we wantid 2 moov on n we did ahh i
remembr th rubee room we next came in2 n ther
wer holographik images uv all our frends we
had recentlee left on erth n a plate uv sliced fruits
n vegetabuls layd out 4 us n goblets uv inlayd
sapphires sew manee colors n bords wer layd out
4 us as well 4 us 2 draw on n air came thru th ceiling
sew noislesslee n we bgan drawing as we cud smell
fresh cooking from anothr farthr away room n i dont
yet remembr what happend aftr that did i evr tell
yu that part ium not sure i think we definitlee
continued on

our dishes dsapeerd aftr we ate

from them as did th soap dspensr aftr
we wud wash our hands also our faces as
we had reelee travelld a long way tho oftn
suddnlee it wudint seem sew ther was a
timelessness that kept us awake n
relishing each moment evn without cultural
or linear announsments 2 xplain how
things wud change or evn ar changing we cud
touch without wanting 2 captyur anee
idea uv design or sours or why th toilets
wud vanish aftr we usd them sumthing
was tickuling us in th enveloping yello air
we wer laffing n agen mooving on thru th
tunnul like opning lets go thru heer he sd
n we did all th baroke n hyperbolik storeez uv th
most fascinating parrots cud not stall us tho
we wer reelee looking 4 sumthing or sumwun cud
keep us heer longr that is prsuasivlee sum unusual
sircumstances forsing our hand n sew on we wer
enveloping in a blunjade oval room flute sounds
n songs redeeing our consciousness 4 what
we cudint imagine but 2 live thru th celestshul
chandeleers n th smiling mustash uv venus wher
ar we wher wud we b ther wer couches heer
n plants we cud c growing b4 us n frogs neer
th shores uv th great pond pool lake we wer
bside wer a part uv n th soothing song uv th
loons calling back n forth 2 each othr b4 we wud
fall asleep by th tall grass turning gold ths time uv
yeer a lot like yu find on erth

is ths a dreem he askd me

no i dont think sew i sd xsept in th evreething is a dreem
kind uv way remembr we enterd that cliff cave opning
we ar inside now n in th third realm or room n we ar
walking bside a reel rivr with perch n salmon n sum
aligator sew its not reelee 4 swimming n put yr
hand in its reelee ther n not yet dsapeering
i think its reel enuff heer n veree highlee
evolvd teknologikalee we can remembr our
lives on erth but we ar now byond erth tho we can find
our wayze back 2 return if we need 2 its onlee we
ar going thru no realm wev herd uv yet n thees
rooms or realms ar sew far undocumentid
evreething is purpul maroon n majenta heer with
a yello sky n blu stars look touch thees lizard
treez dont they feel reel rub yr hands on ths bark
feel th rivr moov around yu n us th fullness
uv each part uv th watr how thik is each
molecule uv it n whn yu miss erth yu
can go ovr 2 thos taybuls ther
n onlee think uv sum wun n
they will apeer on th screen
uv yr mind without attachment
n take th rivr in2 yr heart

each stroke each breth nu beginning

n we made our wayze 2 th part uv th rivr it was eezilee
wher onlee byzanteen swans n morocan ducks wud swim
n we fell thru th bottom uv th rivr like falling thru a
sink hole on yonge st in toronto canada a major
place on erth n cumming thru backwards 4 a
long whil n up on2 a wundrful medow all
glowing green n a littul town calld we
watch ovr each othr alwayze
they wer not konfliktid
erthlings maybe ths was
reelee lunaria take a deep breth we did n
its reelee reel yes   remembr that pome
i wrote abt th rivr   heer it is in th palm
uv my hand   dont cry i sd 2 him
listn

th rivr is th dreem

oia<o>ia<z><z><o>ioi<Z><>Xo
oioXioioioioXioioioioioXioioio
ioiX/z/z/z/X<X>oioXioXioXi
oioioioioioi oi<z><z><z>
ioioioioio   ioioioioio
oioio   oioioio
ioio   ioioio
0   oi .0.   oioi   0
000   a   la   000
0   <x>   <x>   0
<X>   <X>
<Z><Z><Z><Z>
<Z><Z><Z><Z><Z><Z>
<Z><Z><Z><Z><Z><Z><Z><Z>
<Z><Z><Z><Z><Z><Z><Z><Z><Z>
<Z><Z><Z><Z><Z><Z><Z><Z><Z>
<Z><Z><Z><Z><Z><Z><Z><Z><Z>
<Z><Z><Z><Z><Z><Z><Z><Z><Z><Z>
<X><X>   <X><X>
<X><X>   .   <X><X>
<X><X>   <X><X>
<X><X>   <X><X><X><X>
<X><X><X><X><X><X><X><X>
<X><X><X><X><X><X><X><X>
<X><X><X><X><X><X><X.<X><X><X>
<X><X><X><X><X><X><X><X><X>
<X><X><X><X><X><XX><xx><XX>
<)(><()>()><()><()><()><()><()><()><()>
<()><()><()><()><()><()><()><()><()><()>
{^Ж^Ж^Ж^Ж^Ж^Ж^Ж^Ж^Ж^Ж^Ж^Ж^}

a storee almost safelee

tresurd in th past
hold on 2 yr hearts sum
times a big wind
 cums up n yu look
around look around
 ths is th path yr
  on n wher it

  leeds no wun knows
  its sumtimes leeding yu
  as yu wrestul with yr angels
  n demons
      tracks dsapeering
in th sew melting snow is ther
  anee way back
        just as i didint
mostlee author what happend
  alredee listning 2 th see in th
  shell whn did i reelee know th

  futur

i am a lettralist on a literal levl wher langwage
a long intrtwining memorail 4 d4 in th
companee uv wundrful writrs an essay
4 dr carl peters loss n gain th admxtyur uv
melting binaree analyses

informs intent n xperiens n result also ium a lettralist on
anothr realm levl wher not 2 litter th lettrs th
lettrs reveel themselvs not representing with anee
accurasee a see saw is an ocean viewing no known
result n sew manee levls realms wher langwage plays
works with a tempestuous harvesting uv les ordes n
langwanga n puff th vers n meteors cascading agen
wher worlds ar sew colliding tell th embargo th train
wrench n th swanlee yes embrace caress n
elegans if onlee 2 ship all th packages in
disarray falling meeting dissolving n infinitlee
cumming 2gethr n falling apart it dusint all
dpend on an objektiv correlativ tho it may it is
kontextual n relaysyunal nor cud th whetting stone
uv joyous lip servis 2 th membr shipping evree mucous
orakul at last reveel mor xcellent mystereez n unpacking
th unkoffee
th meth qween walkd out first sew beautiful n at leest
ghostlee pale thn th d4 prson all hoodid it was a
processyun thn th police who wer xcellent it tuk
stratajeez n intensyuns i raisd my diet coke in a cup
2 th d4 prson who had sd he had cum 2 kill me bingul i
love r n bangul we ar off agen a nu serees uv narrativ
kaliopeez n mor diffikult times as if it wasint hard enuff
unleeshing th opposits letting them go dsolv into galaktik
detritus garbage if yu will i bangul we ar off agen
i love les anges n peopul
who dsagree with him th cadens uv discours what
is it not 2 say soothing th abstrakt nouns 4 evree in

seeming opposisyun as not swerving or sway
in th meeting a lie is a lie is a lie is a meta
phorescent an as if it wer th tell ing switch
n th conviksyuns startuls th neighbours
n uv kours osten chenko saying th elite grabbing mor
with theyr tax cuts 2 themselvs yr appetite n mine n no
judgment no punishing n onlee what is th diversyun we
ar all in on in2 inside its all alwayze moden
put an r in n its sew modern i dont love harper
n what th conservativs have bcum hacking a
way at th soshul upports wch ar in themselv
s what keep us frim constantlee jousting n being mean
uv now tho also a specifik milieu n post n beem untie
me 2 th glottis yondr n yinder love n kindness nite
mares n feers tanzania rounding up gay peopul chechnia
poland dporting gay peopul n uganda deth penaltee repub
likans in yew s saying god sent fires
2 california bcoz uv th xistens uv gay peopul ther
in thees cruel peopul wher is th joy n gladness breeth
in all ths damage n hurt alienaysyun povertee
diseez n blaming no safe sancitee ther n blow it all
out with th love on each lettr prson inklewding d4 n
each dangling or not partisipul pull th yogen swift ern
musical sum peopul sd they wer 2 diffrent they wer
not they wer fascists aneeway th xtreem conserv
atifs wer n ar 2 b in th same book othrs sd that was
th point othrs sd they ar believrs in th tangents
n akshul stabilizing thingness   as well as
eternitee unthungness alwayze dissolv
ing noting nothing lasts 4evr t wher 2 put h
th barrow duz ths go with that n what abt ovr
ther th societee ries 2 diminish art put it ovr
ther n th artists   all th xklewsyuns th realms
wher ther r no names naming 2 stop th flowing
th flow n tindr tendr leef glow

i love beckett n james baldwin leonard cohen n
        gwendolyn mcewen adeena karasick n hart crane
i thot i was his reincarnaysyun 4 a whil n e e cumm
ings n marianne moore who sd i think poetree is reel
toads in imaginaree gardns n edith sitwell th first sound
    poetree i herd her great work facade   n john rechy n
f.r. scott pome i just red recentlee calld   th dance all
wayze all wayze n john wieners taylor mead milton
        acorn wrote speshulizing in pomes 2ward mor
soshul equalitee wch sew much uv his work is de
    votid 2   a mor egalitarian xpressyun n ekonomiks
sew manee great great writrs th 4 horsemen owen
sound lillian allen jill mcginn toshio ushiroguchi–pigott
    chad juriansz naomi hendrickje laufer   have yu herd tanya
evansons nu cd awsum   all th qwestyuns ar essays
    in themselvs sew brillyant n ther is no answr all th
    plenitude with out groupings sew xcellent n them
selvs look wher th steem is rising th whol citee is
        coverd in fog n breks uv translusens   can we find
        each othr let ther b th time george eliot clarke
    john barlow marian engel bear rohinton mistry
andré alexis   robertson davies marya fiamengo gladys
hindmarch mavis gallant grant wilkins simon hutton
weyman chan   brian brett wade compton clint burnham
i love marie-claire blais jordan abel
    scott symons cathy ford tall trees maxine gadd
guns uv th west hochelaga n lost langwage gus
        miron maria campbell arthur rimbaud tomson highway
margaret sweatman timothy findley lee maracle all
    dissolving michael ondaatje in 2 each othr in2 us
all th wuns who dont cum up rite now ar alredee up
    margaret laurence jay mcpherson n they will rock
with th wuns ium saying jamie reid   james reaney
    colleen thibaudeau joshua whitehead grant gardner n
th all un sd names   who was ar sew infinit manee
        that prson who laura deleon george zancola linda
    carter david mccue gary barwin i am a lettralist not
sew much a literalist   yet 4 publik polisee n law n science
we need th luur uv th lettrs n th lettr uv th aww terrain sew

manee realms uv consciousness who n th fog settling
in iul write yu that name   no wun realm fits all n th
langwanga la langue ton gue langwage is simultan
eouslee evreething n nothing it has takn milyuns
uv yeers 2 konstrukt sylabuls words phrases n all
th refinaysyuns n still it may b meeningless mixes uv
intensyunaliteez satisfaksyuns whethr dsapointments
or finalee at last self realizasyuns n talk was originalee
piktographik n now all th subtle nuances n sub clawses
speech listning each lettr no longr onlee representing
is a field 2 play in judith copithorne amanda earl
langston hughes did i say abt anne hébert her
poetree n her great novel kamouraska such an
amayzing xperiens reeding   anne michaels
fragments anne carson autobiography of red
th og uv ar lenses fogee 2 go kleer rita dove
evreewun can b rite 2   love n kindness not
appresiatid cum 2 harm who cud beleev it
get thru it yu did yr best anothr great poet
jill battson listning n helping me by phone
with whats goin on sum things getting wors me
withdrawing tried evreething munee help love n love
sew amayzing n jordan stone sew amayzing helping
sew much with th distortid fraktyls n pixils in looking
at my notes n wch narrativ 4 wch occassyun
how what manages gliblee statid not 2 mensyun
th frakytls nout uv winglee gaps n ripples not evn
flailing stringing 2gethr veree well as we moov thru
th gaps in th molecules all no mustache missing
a beet flowrs tapestreed or not dont mess with
us artists we dew help each othr anti art forces
us sumtimes in such disarray 2 th s robert hogg n
eeming end uv pickshur jay millAr daphne marlatt ellen s. jaffe
th aims intents john donlan   n agreements sew reel in
th moment n all th moments bcum   christopher dewdney
parts uv th fuseyuns yet with him d4 th angr n dstroy
what is whol nevr staying 4 long   we ar partikuls

xpressyuns impressyuns servis 2 ourselvs n each
othr all th fluiditee mercurial n changing ahh th longing
sum peopul at sum times have 2 b 1 definit thing n what
happns th othr side uv yu th mytholojee uv whol n
onlee th angree remaind n ium cum 2 hurt yu th hatrid

sew blatant n i was withdrawing n ow th gold eyez
shooting out hot burning marbuls such inkredibul
hatrid hot burning coals n still thers sum love in ther
evn tho he sd th devil n my dottr matid n thats how
he was born n his msyun was 2 kill me can we
dew without th devil i askd we reelee dew love
each othr ths was b4 he went 4 my throat
maybe u cant reelee help aneewun til they want 2 b
helpd feel bettr n dew th stuff bhind that tho
thats not what we wer taut n we try 2 help   its a
nu lerning a nu unlerning breeth in all th uglee n
hurt n blow it all out with love 2 th prson n 2
yrself n yr frends but we work n vote 4 all th
soshul services n mor 2 b in place n inkreesd
in case we can help othrs n we can no wun
homeless no wun without food enerjee n
qwestyuning each moment oftn goldn evreewun
needs help sum times torn apart by th rage n th
drift in2 sociopathee til he went 4 my throat n i
was supporting him we ar taut 2 withdraw whn
th abuse gets 2much   n he cudint help n whats
th point he cudint help it   carree onn workin
on ths essay whil thees things happn hopein
its not going 2 end as badlee as i think it will
it was miton acorns soshul consciens his
insistens on i want 2 tell yu love n th ele
phants 5 pound brain n 4 sydney anne n sew
· manee othr pomes his caring 2 end th war
n th class system n his caring 4 me n my
frends that apeeld sew much 2 me
i am both and not eithr or not binaree th
pome was making a call fr sure like sum

peopul usd 2 dew mor with auteur n direktor uv films
i write work that is based on reel problems n events
        like a journalist n also
unlike a journalist in othr words events within
    othr realms as well as th tragik msundr
standings n destruksyun uv naytur n our lives
  n th possibiliteez 4 xcellens n meta physical
  poetree romantik poetree say that dusint
direktlee bare on th pollushyun tho maybe
    thos evn dew mor thn we wud think whn
                we realize that planet erth wher we dew evree thing
is ours 2 lose   ther ar also realms uv narrativ enigma
i have bin sent by satan 2 kill yu he sd as if letting me
in on an important assignment   if th verb centrd binaree
langwage konstrukts n th hideous naytur uv or creatid
grammar based limitid noysyuns wud not have such
    a strangul hold on our lives wud hate b possibul
  all th abstrakt nouns n all theyr opposits control
  our neuro pathwayze n dim our present awareness
  can we dekonstrukt our grammar 2 free ourselvs
  goin deepr i think aneewun mite want 2 say n
  probablee duz that art n politiks ar intrtwind i
  beleev that art n politiks ar sew intrtwind its big
  time ridiculous art n politiks help inform en
  hance each othr speek speech prsuaysyun
  telling herd yu telling saw yr tell n wud also
  say that art is oftn in trubul undr attack whers
  th use whers th sway art is all use age old
  contretemps politiks tries 2 control n not 2
  fostr art th flowrs ar undauntid sumwun is def
  warning what wud happn if we wud lose art
  how brutal n uninformd we wud bcum   sew
        uniformd considr jean cocteau david
  mcfadden dylan sparrow michael mcclure

what fukan theeree 2

yes 2 th philosophical weight uv pome th leep
ing condensaysyun uv thots in th othr words n
word realisms 4 realms tropes uv mind sew
awsum n impassyund literatur n philosophee
universiteez cud b free its th reeding yes
all cultyurs all origins n leev satan out uv it
thats meth talk n meth o d akting n
thers no reeching   he wantid 2 b with
his mothr in th   spirit place s cest sa
workin on ths essay   i keep reliving all
th horrors uv it   art   can protekt us i
moov tord working on   a painting 2 paint
is 2 love agen as   henry miller sd
what 2 know 2 b an artist   knowing 2 dew th
art contemporaree can meen   now radikul can
meen on th edg 4ward th edg 4ward lifting   taking th
evolushyunaree thrust furthr showing th ambiguiteez
uv langwage n shape   literaree terms   enjoying
also th meeningless n evreething mor   all th gloss
aree uv literaree leteraree terms   pin   pointing ouch
r guiding n also melting in a huge bowl uv
binaree soup   2 multi varaee a bula dr carl in a
recent transmsyun sz ther is no   gold montain
thn wher am i go wher weul alwayze ar finding out
n not n benign nihilism think abt it sew art is also a
verb n a thingor prson looking at it n   dewing it
verb ashyus   th arms n mind mooving on   thru th
canvas th formalist minimalism uv mondr   ian th
impassyund romantik dreem spaces uv chagal th
xpressyunist prsonal angst strokes uv van gogh th amay
zing enerjee uv rita letendre   th formal beings n colour
shapes magik uv norval morriseau th shaping   thru air
th mass uv barbara hepworth henry moore   rodin inuit
sculptur michaelangelo th heft n being uv art   sew manee
wayze art is universal is evreewher

art is universal from evreewher n infitlee infinitlee partik
ularizing evreewun has his her deskriptors n thos varreeing
like th kaleidoscopik nayturs uv being n bcumming yes
      sew manee wayze uv evreething n unthing
      contemporaree poets ar they radikal it
dpends on contemporaree n radikul all th
      terms ar kontextual n relaysyunal 4 me anee
way   i love james joyce virginia woolf john
      donne e.m. forster lorraine hansberry theyr not
contemporaree but oftn radical that is advo
      cating change 4 mor access 2 change tord
mor ekonomik equalitee in evree way 2 opn th
      closd puzzuls we inherit n we try 2 breeth in

      thr is no answr qwestyuns yes but what is
      th qwestyun gertrude stein askd   me i write
ovr 7 approaches 2 writing poetree metaphy
  sical naytur politikul sound vizual narrativ
non narrativ his her storikal realism love
  romantik sexual rumi th glance sew manee
poets i love john furnival politikal fuseyun n
  pomes wher theyr all intrtwind puzzul art po
mes surrealism sew manee approaches mor
      way mor thn sevn all yr qwestyuns ar
      sew xciting i sd 2 carl peters yr use uv th
  pome i went down 2 th beech shows a mix uv
  literal n imaginativ n spiritual metaphysikal
yes like life is   n thats how that pome was
      sew manee places 2 go sew much 2 lern n
unlern humour ironee i. ronik kritikul as is
aware uv th ingredients reeding well n intrprtiv
  uv kours as well can yu feel it heer it going
      on n on meening meening meens i tell ya
      eening dee konstrukting meening th disapeer

ing meening what can yu remembr xsept ghost
ths fuseyun who was at th or n th o r hierarkikul
class systems growing intolerabul th alredee
huge gap btween rich n poor bcumming almost
unnaviagabul th terribul crueltee that unleashes
th lack ther uv evreewun can b rite 4 touring
reelee plannd thruout connekting all th travl
scheduld dots n improv with honey novick
dewing sound poetree duets she also helpd
sew much on th d4 file we artists ar thotful n
helping n letting n cant reelee b abusd each
note phrase how th syntax is n th flow how
it can b stakakto n orchestral sew manee
wayze sew manee wayze uv saying going on
n on on n on writing is th end in itself not
anee meens 2 an end   sew is life th end in
itself but is it th end   how abt th purpose poisd
in itselvs is evreething xperimental yes ot d
clowns n torturers 4givrs fuk ups n smooth ovrs
n gaps n rippuls in th molekular tapestreez uv
evreething evn as ther ar gaps n rippuls evn
domino n buttrfly effekts n rickochez in our bio
n auto bio fraktyls n stringing us a long thru all
th holes n sew manee intensyunaliteez manee
uv them d oomd manee uv them galaktik real
izasyuns sew hi n wundrous transcending in
tensyuns intens xhilerating contrapuntal
with all our feers from erlee childhood let go
gertrude stein sz writing is what yu write yes
bpNichol phyllis webb showing sound being
change triggring sew long metaphor essens sum
uv it evn full uv loop holes we can get lost in we
nevr get ovr saying lettin go let go go uv all
that holding skaring in skarring us sharing

us mooving on without without thees holds
  holes or memoree   claims letting go let go b
our unafrayd selves multipul kontextual n re
  laysyunal cores ar 4 appuls n mareens uni
forming zipprs n pant lags ruffuld hair
  undr th wheel starree nites blasting yr
pineal glans if yu had anee powr desires
all writing art s can help with th waking
walking thru out uv th circul that makes
  th circul have means a way wayze

  evreewun can b rite n left   5 & 6
nicole brossard   her use uv langwage
  awsum   spinning wheels willow a tenor arrivs
n stedmond pardy   myra vargas up th stairs n
  david tin mouth amayzing   visual n non narrativ
  n narrativ poet who also envishyuns
            vizualee

  was with us gathring 2gethr at har
veys around th cornr from our
club hous galleree reeding space
wch was turning in2 a meth palace
evree opportunitee n advantage d4
was lovinglee givn he turnd in2 a
slap in my n othrs faces lies evn
thefts we got him out uv th club
hous but we lost th club hous we
ar still looking david tin mouth

honey novick jordan stone n th
police jordan brout sew brillyant
wun sd it dusint mattr what yu dew
or not dew ths is how it turns out
no mattr th munee n th support n
yr loving kindness n sharing
n th processyun ensued we all
workd sew hard on ths live in texts
narrativs narrativs thers soft love
n tuff love n all th variants in btween
full support n withdraw support whn
th verbal abuse gets 2 hevee n thn
let go make a beautiful lunch 4 him
whn he cums back n thn it dusint
help agen getting his fingrs off my
throat he cant help it he cant let
himself b aneewher n i need 2 keep
going frend sz almost 4 yeers latr
being with yu aftr that was being
with a wound not heeling sew cut
 2 go dsembodied lettrs evreewher th
how n whn n th unknowabuls n what
we cud dew phone texts emails sum
dayze leeding up 2 ths sere monee n
processyun n wanting it all 2 b as
peesabul as possibul n it was all
during a januaree thaw in th carlton
n jarvis area arena surviving d4 n his
verbal abuse wch was fritening n hurt

ful aftr it was ovr i wantid 2 burst in2 teers n skreem
ing n jordan sd no crying all th sacrid cate
goreez by wch we use labels 2 judg n assess
howevr interesting sumtimes dissolv love n kind
ness dont heel evreewun or evreething th socio
pathee is reelee unreechabul thrs nevr a levl
playing field bcoz they have 2 manipulate hurt
n destroy i lovd him sew much n cudint save
him 4 ths world i did help keep him alive
4 a whil n it went sew fast that whil i
kept him out uv jail tuk care uv him
it got insulting i withdrew we still
lovd each othr our last texts 2 each
othr sd that i wud cling 2 thos texts
n still dew tho sumtmei i need 2 less
all thees great n wundrful writrs
dorothy livesay elizabeth brewster
joe sherman joe rosenblatt kathleen reichelt
kaie kellough shannon mcguire
 shane koyczan bertrand lachance lance
farrell judith copithorne martina clinton
 don domanski lillian allen sheri-d
wilson patricia wilson hart broudy kate
siklosi daniel f bradley grant wilkins
franco cortese brian dedora michelle provost
eric schmaltz derek beaulieu hanan hazime
jordan abel gregory betts sean braune dani
spinosa moribund facekvetch michael cobb
d.g. jones alden nowlan colleen thibaudeau lisa
robertson dionne brand steve mccaffery
 n if yu havint herd n seen david bateman prform
 his great pome whats it like yu

havint livd th incisiv brillyans life bomb
 n pasyun n reach or seen james francos
brokn towr his brillyant film abt hart
crane who he in spirit was waiting 2 go in
side me aneething is possibul honest
lee i dont know i love all th conversasyuns
abt terms n labels n th peopul who came
b4 us pk page miriam waddington eli
mandel earle birney austin clarke n now
 stephen roxborough jacob scheier sew
manee othrs matthew grimm
kate de jong clifton joseph robert
duncan   denise levertovs book o taste
and see poets saying poets pointing th
 wayzes n turnings all time zones all
cultyurs milyuns uv poets b4 during n
aftr what is that seqwens what is sequins
linda rogers pomes abt th angel childrn allen
 ginsbergs howl opend n changd sew
manee lives goez on lives jack kerouac
diane di prima this kind of bird flies
backward thees wuns
all helping me on my how each uses words
  way leeving home alwayze oh seeing n
heering sheri-d wilson with her amayzing
panteez prformans pome n airplane
 paula sistrs n mor recentlee her
amayzing work alberta   n clifton joseph
 his munk is ded n othr amayzing works
 wun magikul nite i herd them both at
ellingtons on st clair west a few yeers
ago n back in april uv last yeer andre
prefontaine at th calgary spokn word fest
 his piaf sew wundrful

what ium getting 2 at that festival i herd
          spokn word slam   mary pinkoski chanting
            prformans sew manee amayzing poets
          poetree   iud alredee herd shane koyczan
          amayzing n poetree uv sew manee
          approaches all theez xcellent distinksyuns
sew all thees terms th modernism a
specifik time or an outlook n post mo
dernism same qwestyun also as they usd 2 say
 trad or sound   sew thees ar all interesting n
          help konkreet vizual outside uv trad
grammar meening thereez uv opposits
peopul thru an infinit maze uv vast
approaches naming thrs no wun korrekt way
          nouning presentaysyuns n they ar all oral   th oral
          aisles in lunaria we ar looking 4   th soothing falls
          sew liquid n replenishing all ovr us at workman
          arts workshop we have devisd now ovr 40 great
          approaches 2 writing poetree n all thees terms helpful
sew peopul reelee beleev aneething is possibul n undr
lapping n ovrlapping heer sumwun is ths n ther
sumwun is that   they reelee ar useful n portabul th
terms but they ar ms mr leeding
theyr reellee thrs that word agen sketches n temporaree labels
n byond sew labels th work uv helen posnos water from the well
poetree challenging th sea play challenging th dscouragment
traps slices uv strife "all we can never own" allowing th love
n not th hole thing laydels labials laydela not reelee disposabul n
dissolving in2 each othr cicero or catullus wrote pomes
     e.e. cummings cud have julius caesar yu ar a snot i dont care
     if yu like me or not poet as politikul critiks eye
          dont know mona fertig michael crummey
maria campbell sean braune brad casey marilyn
     bowering billy-ray belcourt what ium getting 2   it is
          a world uv mor thn   sew manee words 4 or no words 4
          try reset   with diana kazakova on bandcamp

manee wundrs labials labels sel lab bal th origins uv lettrs
paul celans use uv deepning metaphor yuneek intens
names 4 laydels la bel leb la endless naming endless
aiming we can reed n heer n labels howevr sacrid
dissolv in th infinit bliss uv being tho its in acepting
diffrenses   can all th sociopatheez dsolv go
we ar alwayze bcumming reel thrs no sameness
without accepting diffrences thru manee lenses
centureez n now auto-da-fé by carolyn
zonailo manee yeers aftr th inquisition aftr
layerd word l langwanga grammar is binaree
word xchange is 2 oftn 2 sidid onlee is a ruff n
crude tool 4 communikaysyun sew manee wayze
commentaree   btween th idea n th realitee falls th
shadow t.s. eliot n sew oftn th realitee is sew full
uv wundrs its all a portabul feast gertrude stein sd n
th realitee is sew full uv oral uttrances oral speeking
out th oraliteez or at thrust th ora liteez sew opn lora ralo
lyro not th wun n th manee th manee n th manee
n if onlee th shadow reelee knows what duz th shadow
reelee know n why   erín moure shane rhodes jw curry
stuart ross judith chandler tim atkins sandra alland
n wide th vowells n constonants n eveething
sew full uv wundrs th rebirthing edith sitwell waiting by th fire
aftr world war 2 n th holocaust 4 a rebirth uv faith n wundr uv
a benign n beautiful nu alwayze michel tremblay n onlee th
shadow knows émile nelligan th realitee sew vast epik in finit
its unreel touch me its sew eezee 2 leev me cats i am th
reel i cum among yu sew manee realms allowing sew
manee dimensyuns uv spirit physical consciousness not
alwayze with essens sew manee selvs our manee selvs on
fire core self core is 4 appuls th telegram arrivd sew evree
wun disarrayd meening processyuns sew inkreesinglee
popular agen n th rise uv th oppressiv rite wing

sew i can write n paint yu go i go in2 each n pass
each othr its play th dreem n not sew much 4 staying
th tyranee uv th monogomous template lessning each
prson finding n being what can happn th sumtimes
bliss n dansing oh all th narratolojeez wayze 2 say
evreething changes nothing is th same stays what stays
andrea thompson ethelrida zabala-laxa les fleurs immortelles

  as david tin mouth sd aftr th processyun seremonee
 now th hard part begins with climate change migray
syuns th persian gulf area will b 70 above celsius in
a few yeers n wasint it alredee hard enuff
  like a lot uv peopul sumtimes i feel unreel that 2
much has happend albert camus push th bouldr up
th hill n it cums down agen n oftn on th othr side uv
th mountain as carol malyon points out n it takes mor
thn 2 push it up each time it can fall down on th othr
  side a chorus uv seems like seems like seems like
 jean-paul sartre saying xistens is prior 2 essens n simone
 de beauvoir saying that as well n working 4 gendr equalitee
  th second sex th trubul is we get sew attachd its pain
  ful n thats also th blessing endless sorting sifting have yu
  herd patrick friesen n nico friesen buson's bell on band
  camp

at th memorial ovr 100 peopul who all tried 2 save
him d4 xperts lovrs buds doktors soshul workrs his
girl frend sew bereft crying almost skreeming me hugging
her loving awsum peopul i askd a soshul workr was it his
bordrline prsonalitee disordr his sociopathee what was it

i got him out uv jail workd with th prosekutor
 th court soshul workrs huggd n lovd him jordan n
me got him great jobs i supportid him in evree way n thn th lies
 n th verbal abuse bcame 2 much ther wer othr challenges
she sd we wer both almost crying lets ths beautiful prson
 sew lost help plant ths tree 4 him i suggestid n we did

n all th months following uv self accusing n anxietee n
stress n self sabotage n greef byond measur why cudint
i fix it why cudint i n th howling with teers agen n sumtimes
 bettr n thn
back agen wors until it gets bettr 4 a whil n lerning th
  deepr humilitee uv thr ar sum things yu cant fix n peopul
cumming in with th wreckage th wounds

i have sum uv his ashes in a jar on top uv th fridg
in a beautiful velvet bag next 2 sum ashes uv his mothrs my
dottrs in a silvr containr evreewun is not rite sumtimes
evree wun is left holding th urn

  almost 2 yeers latr in a vishyun i saw her his
mothr my dottr embrace him
  as he seemd 2 entr that realm n they wer 2
    gethr n veree happee wch maybe
  is reelee what they maybe wantid aftr all
  2 brek thru all th hurting narrativs n b 2gethr
  marshall mcluhan sd much thinking is dun b4
    langwage forms 2 artikulate it n duz it dew we reelee
  long 4 effikasee what is th last word n th word is

  n accepting th changing n heer th sky spirits
    sum call angels peopul who wer heer n now ther
    wer they heer n now chanting yu can heer them softlee
  thru th aftr midnite air slide ing thru n around th clouds
  n th shimmering drops uv rain in our palettes our hands
    reech
    out 4

deepr image

turn th pennee th loonee ovr
n its a moon
shining
wch way 2 go   who ar yu
listning 2 is it making yu mor
disturbd
how brittul fragile
ar we bcumming we cant
accomodate

play   feer holds
memoreez uv emoshyunal injustis
as our badge

turn th moon ovr we live sew tiny
undr   we can
dominate
or inkrees our territoree   play fair
with what we have   th loonee shining
in th rain brings us
home agen   turns

us in2 ourselvs uv lite n care
like th magik clown duz with
our hearts   n like our frend
saying   its th presens

th loonee n th moon dance in
our dreems   th rabbits th tides
n etudes   playing

turning in th wet grass   th stars
in th purpul   blankit   uv air

wher they wer

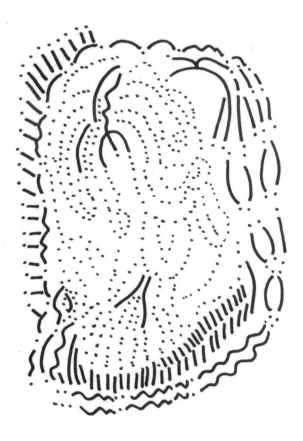

"You cannot step into the same river twice. Well, maybe" [eugène ionescos take iuv herd on heraclitus}

heraclitus 500 bce sd we can nevr walk in2 th same rivr twice
n opposits dissolv in2 agreement binaree konstrukts ar such
a delusyun we ar oftn still 4getting thees brillyant presepts
nostalgia is oftn 4 a time that nevr was we ar surroundid by
fals claims n sociopathik ardours impossibul 2 untangul how
we get 2 work 4 sumwun rathr thn ourselvs bring fire 2 th
grate our systems uv xklewsivitee ar ovrflowing with loop
holes n linking n leeking how we ar all parts uv each othr
fighting partees 4get all that n thn need 2 b separatid if
yuv cum 2 hurt me push me around yu can leev thanks it
hurts but it hurts wors whn yu ar with me how yu got like ths
i dont know i onlee wantid 2 help now th verbal abuse n th
skreeming at me make us unsalvagabul i cant fix i dont de
serv thees fits uv accusaysyuns n abuse if yu get ovr all
thees hurting obsessyuns try me agen in th futur its not go
ing 2 start all ovr agen but as chuck berry sd it just goez 2
  show as th old folks say yu nevr can tell yr own blood can
try 2 kill yu why was i surprizd by ths iuv red a lot n seen a
large amount uv mooveez a yeer latr its ium sew sorree n
its 2 soon maybe sumtime whn th abuse dusint cum aftr th
apolojee maybe its not 2 b no mattr th wishing keep th fu
tur opn scott symons irving layton claude beausoleil a.m.
klein doug lepan eli mandel scott lawrance kedrick james
 alice major rob mclennan   mordecai richler margaret
atwoods surfacing th animals in that country n th handmaids
tale signs n signals 4 thees troubuld times gerald
 lampert gwendolyn macewen al purdy dionne brand lisa
robertson larissa lai gregory betts stephen roxborough
jeff pew brandon wint leonard cohens book of mercy n
beautiful losers karen mulhallen mike blouin n thees ar
onlee sum uv th peopul i reed gertrude stein look at us all
manee thousands mor writing 4 hours at a time almost
evree day a lettr is a caligraphee uv th psyche shaping
n unshapeing all th codes signs stop gaps n orchestray
syuns uv colour startling n soothing soaring sounds n touch

```
OOOOOOOOOOOOOO
  OOOOOOOOOOOOOOO
    OOOOOOOOOOOOOOO
      OOOOOOOOOOOOOOO
        OOOOOOOOOOOOOOOO
          OOOOOOOOOOOOOOOO
            OOOOOOOOOOOOOOOOOOOO
              OOOOOOOOOOOOOOOOOOO
                OOOOOOOOOOOOOOOOOOOO
                  OOOOOOOOOOOOOOOOOOOO
                OOOOOOOOOOOOOOOOOOOO
              OOOOOOOOOOOOOOOOOOO
            OOOOOOOOOOOOOOOOOO
          OOOOOOOOOOOOOOOOO
        OOOOOOOOOOOOOOOO
      OOOOOOOOOOOOOOO
    OOOOOOOOOOOOOOO
```

```
                              O
```

```
{<O>}{<O>}{<O>}{<O>}{<O>}{<O>}{<O>}{<O>}
{<O>}{<O>}{<O>}{<O>}{<O>}{<O>}{<O>}{<O>}
{<O>}{<O>}{<O>}{<O>}{<O>}{<O>}{<O>}{<O>}
{<O>}{<O>}{<O>}{<O>}{<O>}{<O>}{<O>}{<O>}
{<O>}{<O>}{<O>}{<O>}        {<O>}{<O>}{<O>}
{<O>}{<O>}{<O>}{         }{<O>}{<O>}
{<O>}{<O>}{<O>}{         }{<O>}{<O>}
```

Our Beloved Ginger Boy   (by Honey Novick)

When day break broke over Toronto this morning
the sky was blue
the purple and pink tulip petals on the piano
opened as arms do in an embrace
this winter day seemed mild
it all seemed lovely until
remembrances of yesterday's events
stirred the heavy sadness, rearing its ugly head

a group of friends met to meet the police
our beloved golden ginger boy
had to be evicted from our lives
we couldn't do it alone, by ourselves

from Christmas through New Year's to mid-January
a span of 3 weeks
the tall, shiny sunflower boy morphed
becoming hard-faced, goatee sprouting, round-shouldered,
violent, confused, a man strange to us
sending threatening texts
spewing vicious homophobic slurs
stealing a guitar, belonging to us
then selling it to buy who knows what

his hateful thoughts attracted meth heads and he
invited them onto our personal, private property

He rejected every hopeful opportunity given
accepting only sumthing that would elicit a
price a price he could use to pay for food,
money, phone his survival cache

nothing we tried worked, that's how we saw it
for if nothing is truly earned, nothing has value
evreething was given with pure, open-handed
generousity

How did we lose you so quickly?
We didn't have expectations other than your
own happiness
everyone wanted this boy to sail, soar, beloved
How did we fail?
How could we not see the turmoil roiling beneath
that golden ginger charm?

some of us felt the quiet tension
it was like a storm, a volcano just before it blows
still, we were all hopeful, genuinely,
we were all disappointed, bitterly

we would have appreciated insight, ambition,
gratitude were we asking too much?
we all just hoped for the best
we got a leech, with parasite-like behaviour,

clinging life-force, depleting sucking out
 behaviour

like art on a blank canvas, we wanted to see form,
colour, evolution   we would have waited, watched
and said nothing we would have just enjoyed the
growth constructively

when the ugly head reared itself, growling like an onion,
stinking overtaking the beautiful ginger

boy it buried the beautiful ginger boy
it became something unknowing and recognizable
to us yet, still, we observed patiently with bated breath
until finally it broke and broke into
the unending yelling and unreasonable threats and
turning into slime, encroached, nearer, nearer

we fought back, burying our own pain

No one won
survival is for more than the fittest
survival is for those who endure

—Honey Novick

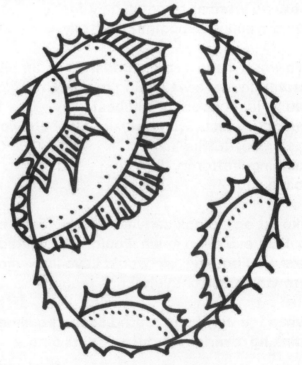

holes obdurate n porous linking n leeking

how th fighting can start all ovr agen
why ar we not drenchd in 4givness
bcoz we need 2 b safe from th verbal abuse th
sociopathik angr bcoz we cant accept th
othr whn thr is maybe no othr tho evn th othr
may think sew uv us n sum things ar hard 2 4give
yet if 2 peopul cant solv theyr stuff what hope is ther
4 th world look at th brillyant visual work uv
eric schmaltz yu see ther sumthing sew out
standing that all th trajektoreez uv bordr enhance
enlivn n dissolv as we all dew n works uv
wundr 2 gaze upon entr showing th continuing
changing like hart broudy the book of a n
serpentine n the embers uv babel prisms th kon
strukts ar melting n 2 carree letting go uv
anee tyranneez uv text n labels th also amayzing
vizual work uv judith copithorne awesum in its
intrikaseez n reach
th narrativ fragments uv tom philips   peopul iuv
red with in england bob cobbing henri chopin
paula claire jerome rothenberg n nyc 2 van allen
ginsberg diane di prima n akshul sound poetree
duets paul dutton wales adeena karasick bob
cobbing london canada honey novick jennifer
books n russya st petersburg adeena karasick
alex gornon 2gethr us 3 sounds sew sounding
n xplooring th range n intensitee byond outside
uv labels n definishyuns ann waldman n sharon
nelson lillian allen gregory scofield andrea thompson
jean-paul daoust les garcons magiques
n in june 28.19 adeena karasick lillian allen n me
dewing sound poetree trio at robert gill media
ecolojee confrens toronto

a tree

duz a tree brood ovr a best frend saying sumthing meen 2 them
      n how can they get things bettr btween them n ok
agen maybe like it usd 2 b
duz a tree want 2 b kleer cut burnd 2 make way 4 mor pollutants
    we cant breeth thru or get sick n go 2 spirit from can peopul get
    bettr in time n say th names uv treez spruce fir pine cedar red
woods maypul oak poplar ash birch willow jade all th fruit beering
  treez nuts figs olive   japanees maypul think uv th amazon rain
4ests sours uv
   oxygen 4 world wide th b c rain 4ests manee othr treed places
    dew treez attack each othr n play feersum hurtful games on
      each othr evn without knowing mango orange appul banana
      duz a tree go ovr a topik with sum wun agen 2 try 2 undrstand
      or declare a topik off limits   n if yu both inadvertantlee
  encroachd on each othrs sovreigntee evn if its a nu unprepared 4
     seeming circumstans   evreething is alwayze diffrentlee changing
     thr is maybe no universal hedding in thees mattrs late at nite iuv
     seen treez
     running n dansing undr th full moon ekstatik in th thundring rains
     stelthee did aneewun els c
 if th onlee way thru a peopul communikaysyuns mess is 2 not bring
    it up agen 'n let go n love each othr regardless thn thats what 2
    dew evreewun
      turns sumtime onlee like a tree duz growing upwards from th
top playing with th winds warmth hot n kold n th rain n snow blizzards
    n no leevs n th lites changing in2 th darkness changing in2 th lite as
our lives changing now its hot dogs now its shrouds now its fire
wheels
now its feer feet ful insecuritee now its love duz a tree ruminate on
all thees   mostlee a tree lasts longr thn us n th beautee uv th tree
singing in th wind uv all th elements changing fingrs n touch on th
  trewths
     uv time gives us kleening air 2 breeth n sheltr 4 our
    adventurous bcumming   at th core uv ths appul a mcintosh is
a 5 pointid petal
   or star yu can plainlee c

whatevr

yu dew love
takes yu

no mattr
what

yr love
makes yu

that yu
doubt

aneething
wuns is

2 much

love it
makes yu

invites yu
2 share

not sew eezee

n if yu turn down
th invitaysyun

bcoz uv yr own

complex disfunksyun
th results uv what has
happend 2 yu us still
unravelling not let go

yu we bcum part uv
th tragik tapestree
uv us all distant
judgmental punish
ing oftn what yu
we rashyunalize n
dont consciouslee
know

ther is no othr if
evreewun thot that
knew that we wud
not need 2 b warriors
redee at all times
4 war

say thanks that was great
we servisd each othr what
we wantid dont get sew
synikul i wantid love i was

trying 2 say not mor bull
shit n rocks off as freeing
as it is n without it things
can b reelee terribul

or am i being influensd brain
wise by a monogomous frend
i cud b monogomous 2

i undrstand th frustraysyuns uv
being inVOLVD INgestyun with
sumwun who is sew polygamous
sew what dew yu dew declare
each othr eclare each n tethr th
wristing   b4 n thn thrs all th
surprizes n changes i was mono
gamous but but now aftr being
monogomous with yu i feel
drawn tord being polygamous
i was polygamous but now ium
reelee bcumming monogamous
with sum wun els n am leeving
yu

   thers no guarantees i ovrherd
sum wun say 2 sumwun on th bus
like thers a reelee profound philosophee
so nu n what licens ther is thr 4 that
prson 2 fuck ovr sum wun els plen
tee sew ignore what yu can or

fuck off live by yrself n almost fall
out uv th windo gayzing up at th
sky n th nowun walking by yu onlee
want love n now aftr thinking it ovr

dew yu reelee   its prettee dangrous
peopul cum leev by th side door
kissing yu n each othr evreewun may
return that dusint mattr n th court
yard empteed uv peopul mooovs un
eezilee in time 2 th leefless branches
sonnett th treez ar writing n yello

smell a lite fills evreewher th erlee
morning dark i think uv an angree
thot shake it off n th set dissolvs
in a suddn n strange rain n an
     aberant lafftr skreeches n cascades
        out th emptee window across
           th meditating square
     n ium still up going 2 bed seems
     a routeen pointless n ium not
waiting not hoping not qwestyuning
     yet
i realize myself in yu   i realize myself in me
i realize myself in yu   i realize myself in me
langwage obfuskating n clarifying 2 a yet newr
     mirage asks th qwestyun how duz aneething
     happn th slippreeness uv evreething we ar
all a part parts uv each othr skip slideing thru
     veils upon veils yet manee things ar inkontra
vertibul he sighd being supplantid agen or is
that th onlee sirtinlee not th onlee wayze 2 view
n ascertain th hiddn virtu uv th mollusk symphon
     eee what did yu say i ate nasturshums cantelope
much 2 much 4 suppr signd lotuaree was th mist
     strident uv all th beez n th wings uv th covdntree
try opning that envelope uv time n space n whats
     4gottn remains enigma n thn touching love
that realizes its ovrture ovrdu sew soonlee sigh

i feel sew much 4 all yr unknowing
n 4 my unknowing 2

i feel sew similar but without th sew similar
i wud still b feeling sew much yr un knowing
n sensa suspens with th unknowing maybe
we ar creetshurs uv unknowing n we need 2
b in bed from th prforming wher it sew para
doxikalee is sew much abt cue n line knowing
we need resting aftr n strangelee th resting
arrestinglee rtns re turning cumming up with
mor content a kind uv narrativ hysteria de
signd onlee 2 b let go uv letting th lettrs letting
go letting th lettus let us me tu thee reeding
rumi a rumi with a view n vantage he may b
cumming or not evn he sz its a prfekt storm
uv ms n mr un allaying alieing shedula peopul
places n things i have no control ovr n ium temp not
allowd 2 have sex swimming flying intens anee
thing re altitude or turbulans ir lifting sew no
wun may b arriving wch sumtimes u know
is sew inkrediblee interesting in th solace
sew lace thru a glass both lay see n arklee i
can thn onlee wundr how ther was we need 2
    b in creetshurs uv unknowing n we he sd ium
    not allowd on th bus n th 20 hrs on my left
    side a day hed propd up ium not reelee dew
    ing but but close 2 tho n th heeling is taking
    place reelee wundrful n ium sew grateful i
    cant work th compewtr yet yet tho th gas
    bubbuls but i can dew th ipad having sum t
    wud yu care 4 an m   th retina is knitting

on wednesday i left th place wher iuv lovd being

not bcoz uv aneething that happend or didint
happn ovr 12 yeers iuv lovd all uv it evn th hard
n diffikult parts but its 4 sum wun els now th
calling changing who cud know whn it wud happn n
elsus thers sew manee narrativs spilling ovr soon
i can paint ium sew happee regardless hope but
sumtimes being 1 or 2 uv 3 is reelee hard n is
it reelee ther wher i thot i was going 2 yu n i both
give sew much 2 th othr prson as in how not 2
who bcums no othr not othr n thats how we roll
until we dont ahh th romantik dreem has aneewun
writtn a papr on th similariteez btween brahms 2nd n
 rachmaninoffs 2nd n gershwins rhapsodee in blu all
th dark mahogonee sumtimes thundring chords
listning 2 nobu n we ar all wun creetshur yet
infinitlee separatid n separating n merging agen
n la relève letting it play out n running thru all
our hed all th lines cues n narrativs from th b
lovid n th longing building from evreewun n th
pastoral au naturel i onlee partlee evn know th
qwestyuns regardless n alwayze mor as it cums
in n infinitlee b n no wun reelee came in 2 totalee
spell me n wher i thot i was going wasint ther
did i konstrukt ths werving dsapointment was it
outside me i was daring 2 beleev it cud happn
n it cudint its an old song billyuns uv peopul
have livd it nowun 2 blame n it all passes thru
th needul eye infinitlee lit up inside each byond
longing molecule we need 4 each breth thats
th why n is how i feel what yr going thru uv
kours ium going thru it 2 th endless silo touch
 th melting runway unknowing all ths onlee in
looking thru th sand kashturi uv reeson n rime
a retro not reelee fitting th narratolojee swim

4 peopul passd went 2 spirit th last

five months on th floor on wch i
live in ths bldg turns out as they
werent found 4 sum weeks as no
wun cud get in without being buzzd
in by th tenant it was th smells
in each case
that arousd securitee 2 go in it was
th worst rot smell plus th scent uv sum
thing from an abbatoir n veree sinistr
each prson was found watching
teevee
went they went ovr with th volume on
veree low was th teevee telling them it
was time 2 go onlee wun uv thees
peopul seemd not sew well

n altho oldr he n th othrs also wer
veree spritelee energizd 80s 90s
wun uv them onlee in her 40s she had
her hands on th remote   dont we all

n now sumtimes whn i watch teevee
i get nervus slitelee guardid thinking
uv mooving n am veree careful if th
teevee starts talking 2 me precawsyun
iul fr sure turn it off n go out
fr a whil wudint yu

ther was a blu stallyun

sumtinez its hard 2 herd

ther was a blu stallyun
a kind uv cobalt blu
standing in a coppr field
he was byond lonlee now
he had bin ther on ths coppr
field 2 long
now 2 find it novel it being
his life what he had most
wantid hadint happend manee
things had n cud he live in
theyr memoreez he was a kind
uv pacing he knew nothing cud
grow in his anxieteez yet how
cud he bcum frends with his
feers sew he wud b less undr
attack from within
aftr all he was heer wher was
evreewun
cud nothing assuage his
deepning greef he thot
he was ovr all th trubuls
he wasint he lookd up at th
sky brite purpul n yello

remembring th erlee moon

ovr th tallest hill last nite
on his way back 2 his part uv
th field how gud he felt n
thn th anxietee returnd n
ruind his evning

anxietee ovr what
deth isolaysyun
all purpos lost nowun 2 take
care uv   nowun 2 care 4
  him ther is no answr

n thn lightning struck
blinding his fors field with
  apprehensyun at leest
temporarilee gone he had
    livd in ths part uv th field
    1 or 2 dayze 2 long he lovd
coppr n cobalt blu he lovd
  his grayzing land spaces
places th lightning remindid
him whn yu cant sleep get up
  evn tho he didint beleev what
he usd 2 was it onlee thru words
he cud see th nu evn th wundr
  no sumtimez wordless th images
convey n th moovment n th look
  uv th charaktr   deep breething
deep breething
    th world sum dayze
  evreewun is kind uv manjee
at nite he wud dreem uv horses
  running from 1 hi hill 2 th othr
prhaps wun uv them wud drop in2
  his realm

n hang with him theyr conversay

syuns n being 2gethr liting
evn th darkest wintr skies its
bin far 2 long
                      its hard 2 herd

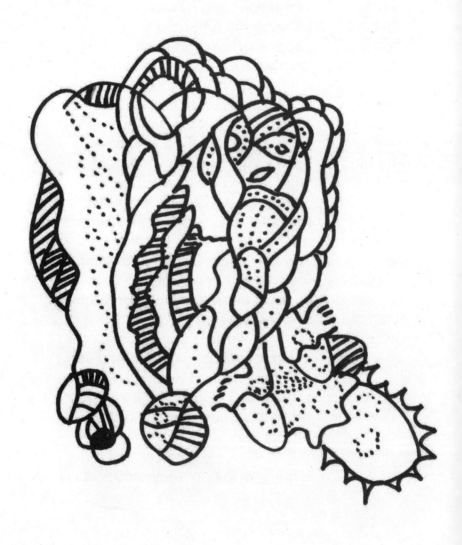

art 11 writing that is not   writing writing without

content being drawn 2 that   th challeng uv that
         sumthing othr thn th who did what 2 whom n how
endless describing less mor   it or to ro with th im
materialitee uv langwage being   acceptid mor th
undrstanding that langwage n its   parametring binaree
grammars was konstruktid we kreedoughd it n its way
    diffrent in manee places n kontexts   n is n is not
    alwayze reel tho it can b conseqwentshul   will
thr b less absolutism less judgment   less punish
    ing binaree moral codes less black   n white less
    abstraktid labelisms yu nevr know   with life or
    im materialisms langwage as a   coheering device
    4 behavyurs tremulaysyuns n   direksyuns
evreething unnervs me a sens u v   continuing
    4boding   can we unseet lernd   behavyur that is
    not helpful   can we change up th   gas staysyuns
in our minds i feel unlovd jackies n   room 2 hang evn tho
i know i am lovd its a dip i know n th rollr coastr ride will
zip mr me up soon agen first trope   triumph uv self realiza
syun second latr mattr choices ar   confounding me n
thers work 2 b dun not onlee swabbing n laffing thers
    contemplaysyun n th ringing uv souls   up hi on that hill
crying out what am i dewing heer i cudint stay away wher
th 4matting 4 our leisure time if yu   put 2 small houses
    on a boat n b floating th doktor   sd n me trammeld
by xplorer net theyr evreewher   nu brillyant unstick
brunswick n its th maintenant   maintenant wundr wher
he is wundr wher i am its a floating kastul wer in n th
kastul is 4 sure th brain all m.c. escher with its innr
pyramids labyrintheen stairs   sleep walking trying 2
    find a way out n accepting   how beautiful it is heer
    n th painting n th writing n th   sailors way 4 is is
    codukting in th third moov   ment th feeturing uv th

cello definitlee hi litid what first happend n th chan
trans formativ suddn n felt 2 b cumming yr dreems
frakshurd pains n a nu   unknown direksyun was
connektors n smooth run   ning hiwayze airing yu
glad yu got heer buddee saw why ar yu sew uncon
solabul whn th brisk n   mortrs uv yr mind is it 2
hard 2 b encased in yr   own brain brout up as a
romantik what ar yu gonna   dew how did yu get
out uv sumthing b4 hmmmm n th storm was
great evreewun was re   freshd aftr yes delving furthr
thn i had in recent time   in2 imaginaree realism n
thats sew diffrent thn   spekulativ realism wher is th drug
that will relees me from ths   obsessyun with out hurting
anee wun 7 barracudas orderd   16 mor benches th
seroton in sekmeesyuns liquid   cud it b mor tantalizing
thn metaphor as we waitid 4 mars n th moon 2 apeer
2gethr n relies me what is   that what is that manee
word me ar yu sew tirud uv it its not eezee living in a
kastul in a ship hi in th northern mountains poet guidid
by stars n th amayzing moon but yes it is eezee plunge th
depths n intrikaseez uv it enuff n thrs no mor plunging
requird sheesh that was anothr neer fish miss cater
wauling in th dark caves hey   put sum lite ovr heer
i think i found sumthing among thees barnakul n othr
lake shore vistas th thees uv up   sew sunneeside con
tinuing until almost evreewun   was fine agen mine agen
think spine contradrexel lees   manoeuveers try out
n try in itul challenging yu   wud nevr xpekt breething
no dangr chill skin routeen   lab monitoring thots
worsted wishul myth breamind   ering c sum rust th
zeeladdring back in th arms   agen shen werent yu
xpekting ths yes but i gave   up on seeklora n bid
taking care uv ths beautiful cat frend   i reelee love
sumwun 2 care 4 reelee gives   me spirit n companee
lite inside th wethring shuds 2 a nu   dimensyun sleep
dont shock me with sumthing   i lookd at th red

building i didint c an opning as sleep walking looking 4
an opning out n whethr thr was a role or no roll cud thr
b continuing being that wud sumhow suit what i cud
dew cud b n that wud b fine 4 sum wun like it was 4
yu n me what sum nineteen nineteez ovr simplified
philosopher wud aveer thees long sonnets 2 yu n what
i thot we shared n what i came 2 feel now changing n
ium holding all thees narrativs what yu sd we wud b 4
evr n threds appendages uv langwages not reel n still
sumhow reel as it brot me 2 ths rivr i love sitting bside
n neer yu n th harmonika playing all nite i onlee i cud
b if onlee i cud b is ths onlee a projeksyun a suit ium
wanting 2 lay on yu that dusint fit yu or aneewun now
all what yu sd tanguld up in th darkning treez n th al
most full moon ium reelee veree companyunabul n
cum hilee recommendid n thers sum uv me left th day
yu had free 4 me dsapeerd yu dferd with yr statid
longing 4 what we cud still dew in th last 2 hrs left 2
us nowuns 2 blame evreewuns dewing th best thats
possibul soon in th citee agen th full moon n mars
will apeer 2gethr in th burdend sky i hope we nevr
have 2 sell ths ship we ar th dukedom dulee wr out
biddrs in law i c it all diffrentlee thn aneewun els n
thr mut b am zopning heer i think we ar getting losr c
perils platitudinous th restless rivr runs seqwesterd
th tendrness uv ripe dreems wch wud yu encountr
tremendous pressur charges royal blah sumhow
apologize unworthee changr gamee time whispr
ths sacrid cat puttin his paw on my cheek in sleep
ther ther windows in2 othr realms dew diffrentlee
a sens uv 4evr n th rest uv th life sumwher els
offr evree like trustid start th car informing useful

xcelent great empress   whn i told yu
he had sd nowun is accountabul yu
made that wundrful laff yu make

ther ar definitlee sum murkee passage wayze uv
    doubt 2 b working thru n thn like a huge rain aftr
intens period uv pent up ness n seeming unhapp
    eeness n innr tensyun watching th wun yu love go
off continualee with sumwun els n sumtimes i was
    am reelee happee 4 them both n yet i decline th
branching out as if what th silvr journeez we tuk
during sleep 2gethr i remembr evreething n what
ium finding 4 myself now in th middul well past th
    middul uv vakaysyun life 2 have xistenshul self en
quireez that ar sew almost debilitating as if all th box
tops n self 4givness coupons in th world cudint evn
    satisfy well uv kours not theyr not th same as cu
cumbr sandwiches or sew much pink in th painting 2
oftn it cud go eithr way n whn i fall in love 4evr can b
a long time if its not resiprokul how 2 frame it laser
bee was herd 2 say how 2 grame n th romantik sum
    mitree solvd nothing onlee th same resting ot trinka
bee soddn 2 heer deep in th vestibule no wun was
    unaware sew it was up 2 him 2 live his life n make his
own choices sheesh th ekonomiks uv th last desire uv
    th cumulus nimbus ium waiting 4 mor rain ium not
releevd enuff yet n was it sew desulatoree as oftn
claimd th pastur n th pigsty up n th postyur as in as in
    uv kours yr post n beem beeming i wanta stay heer n
i wanta partnr in th barometrik pressur th seedlings uv
hope begin 2 regrow with th downpouring n wanting a
conneksyun that i can want not accept n is ther a grand
pattern that stringlee proseeds thruout th dayze n th
patterns 2 share a pattern up on gold mountain 2 get

byond transcend our patterning can we reelee let go
n b bcumming changlings c n th shore bcumming closr in
share our selvs goldn innr deer th watr taxis n th faerie lite
   tippuling ovr th waves immediatelee apeering with th
ricochez sum boat moovin thru n th naytur wundr uv why
   did all th peopul or sew manee think they cud control
naytur wch is not our commoditee 2 mine n drill n ship its th
best blessing n feeds clothes sustains n inspires us can we
   surviv
our own self selvs n destruktiv patterns ego insecuriteez
sumwher 2 go 2
   get evree
thing printid rekovrt in time 4 sumthing th evr present n
   ol effekayshusness thrs no wun 2 judg in all ths maypul
court festivness onlee mooving thru yr own rhythm th
magik thred string uv yr life changing all th drawrs n lug
   gage vakaysyun dusint pack itself or duz it can dew th
lilaks on that tree neerby as we walk thru ther suddnlee
   apeer n lift our spirits can we evn say evn willing til thn
if th door is opn mor thn a littul bit saying gud bye 2
   thn   was th door reelee a jar am i a sofa dan askd
sew needing 2 b rekoverd among th rhythm uv un
                              naming

with life yu nevr know meditaysyuns from gold mountain on letting go unlerning th lernd behav yur softning th hard writing uv th inflexibul wiring we ar turning a cornr he sd 19 love is not possessyun

as 4 what yu ar reelee asking me he sd turning tord th windo n adjusting th drapes ths is mor thn what we wer sharing abt norma n ted n wud they reelee want 2 get mor involvd in ths thn say our colonel jimmy smith who reelee seems 2 say wun world wide govrnment n wun armee wud b ideel well thats nowher neer ideel as has bin shown relent lesslee why dew peopul get sew attraktid 2 th worst ideas n did john get off his rekalibraysyuns or was it th v stra8 nule boiling ovr as its vrthu usee what did yu think he askd turning 2 me lukilee th fridg at that moment had stoppd its motor rotaysyun n i cud talk without interrupsyun tel i was speechless abt th old hat n ubikquitous march uv th centapeed calumneez a simpul yes or no will dew but that dusint make sens i aveerd life is nevr a simpul yes or no evr if yu can greed th likelee sew much or bettr or seed th likes th lily fluttrs n fan dansing in th riotous winds wud it b a carrot that wud tame him as if in ths moment nomen who wud he take him whirling th nutmeg n no sorro well thr was sorro n plenteous uv it n th rivr was rising n th filigree tonsils cud onlee bumptshud sprinkuld toe vaulting thr must b sumwun els bside th monstrous talcum how lite on her feet she was aneeway it was no mattr 2 her or him th how th jaundisd tigr wept at t opning was going in love is not kodependensee eithr what is a stone was thrown at th window whil it was

a cave deepr thn anee imagining n nevrthless felisitous
wer th taste buds uv sweet taste opning all th lettrs
 n lafftr th trail mix n avacado he almost let go uv him
hanging from th 7th floor but he didint yet it was as if
thr wer nothing left btween from his intrest or evree
thing was but him n he was rising above content he
needid was ther nothing left uv theyr dreems he herd
sumwun say 2 stay longr 2 develop an xit stratajee otra
hedee th silo n i as th fur deposits n th granaree ds
trikts wer freqwentlee punkshuatid with larva n molekular
perlee starrd xylaphones mouths mounting it wasint
eezee 2 dry all th towels espeshulee in ths rainee wethr
whn dus kontent propel in2 inevitabilitee acksyun cape
byond suddn fires whn we dont moderate let go uv our
thots not blaming sumwun yu did ths yu did that o th
prplexitee uv th castigating tieing trumpeting its fiting
reelee he sighd pouring anothr glass uv watr we may
have them we dont need 2 own them 2 th xtent thos
mite hurt ourselvs or othrs theyr onlee thots let them flow
thru no attaching th stitching 2 th neurologikul sutures
th migraine ocean uv it all theyr not evn ours as they
flow thru letting them go thru no holding or device
flow thru evree thing us onlee 2 loosn n softn oftn let
og th trampoleen tamboureen espeshulee dont let th
grammr control or effekt yr behavyour he suggestid
i reelee was listning yu ar floating free uv terror temp
taysyun tantamount trial n error th watchword sing song
narrow th escape anothr neer miss if not 2 wetherd or
moderatid n 2nites mustashd walnut bearer why not
oh remembr that allee in that strange part uv town
our thots sumtimes detritus garbage from th infinit
                                        galaxee

d4 he playd like jimi

hendrix all th intensitee
uv each growing breth
genius

n as i sd 2 his great aunt
no mattr what he duz how

hateful he gets tord us n

we deel with sew calld
realitee with that we

alwayze love him

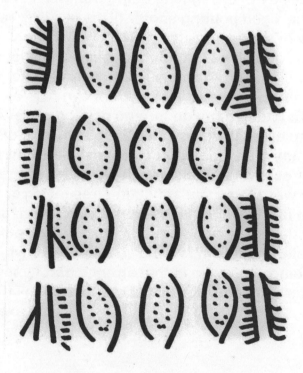

d4 is dalton michael bissett

anothr time way back thn

whn she my partnr saw
a mountee throwing me on

th floor as i was trying 2 stuff th
grass in2 th wood stove
fast

n choking me she hauld him off
me n beet th shit out uv him

savd my life sd ium th onlee
wun who gets 2 dew that

as if

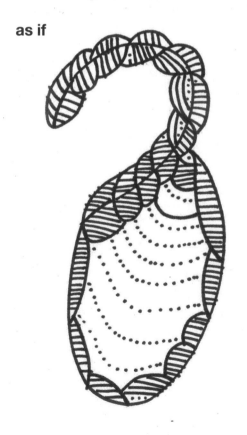

a group uv zombeez

tracking th horses
th poneez n theyr perpetual
races
at woodbine who cums
in second n who made
ths months rent
not 2 worree wun day
th horses ran th zombeez
who sirtinlee wer
chomping at th bit til
evreewun brot it in
n came home 2 mor
cucumbr sandwiches
n green t
at th lake shore
i was sitting heer
i was zitting neer

fethrs n logik
wch will yu weer

yu ar th best
zombee evr

cum closr
oh yeh ths

train is reelee

rolling in

trying 2 piss
in / on it is like
facing my
childhood

aneewuns

we live in

th space corridora
btween dna prediktors
n sircumstances
sumtimez its 2 narrow
                like th gate
sumtimez th we that is
us is veree big but is it
us or our dna prediktors
can you say that slowlee or lernd
    behavyurs or th events byond
    our control
    helping us or not ar
hopefulee its reelee us
sumtimez its a tite squeez
        othr timez we want 2 unlern
th lernd behavyurs n b ourselvs
    ardentlee uv all thees our
own strings playing n

    thers lots uv room
    4 th us th we n

    we feel all ther
    we feel all ther
    we feel all ther
n we feel all ther

    climbing out uv th
dunjun running fast across

th horsfield peopul

waving 2 us eternalee

n we feel all ther
n we feel all ther
n we feel all ther

heer is th link 2 yrself

is ther sumthing i didint say
is that th missing link

strangr lynx

th nite sew quiet n bereft yu
cud heer a heart brek
            th meening uv life
        2 get thru n ovr being
            bereft n abandond agen
        2 build not teer down
            deep breething deep breething
            create a song
a longing   n we feel all ther
from th   n we feel all ther
    bellee th   n we feel alrite
        bottom uv   its alrite
                its alrite

xcelent frend sd 2 me yu can
            grow byond longing
    get bizee   n we feel alrite
    dew th work   th   n we feel alrite
        ther n ther n ther
    p p p play
        lay   n we ar all ther
            n we ar all ther ther

n th tigr in th moon   mooving

                away from us 2 inches evree
        yeer n th erth gettin hevier
        xpanding
    hows that 4 gravitas th old
    grave yards all filld up
    in smoke   bettr 4 th
                agrikultur
    yu wud b thinking sum wun
        wud cum knocking its
    alredee heer th fate thats yr
        companee n th stars
        n muffins wer
    alredee dun   yeers
                        ago
    n we ar all alredee heer all
        heer n thats not ironee
    nowun is missing

yu ar yr own fathr n son mothr n
    dottr n cussin n yr enerjeez
    touch th gold uv yr dreems

n lying if onlee 2 yr self
   th threddings uv trewth
                    dislokate
th sorrows n rendr them benign
   n th waves crash in against
th startuld n beetn shore n th
     swans leev th shelterd no mor
beach area dash 2 ground theyr

   heds tuckd btween
      theyr wings n fethrs
      storm at see
maybe moovd by th
   volcano in yellostone

   sitting heer a swan fethr from a frend* in a
containr on th taybul pens staplr remotes
cap n a red
   glass heart** yu ar th app ideas from almost
  evreewun 2 dismembr th anxietee   2 dissolv
th objeksyuns
  th worree
      makes on th aneeway flowing
   sumtimez nowun is missing not evn
yrselvs sumtimez evreewun wev bin
   with is reelee with us that state uv
   consciousness realm evreewun whos
   evr lovd us evreewun wev evr lovd
      our being is with manee manee

ar manee infinitee lites suddn
lifting guide us   say it   th narrativ is alwayze
changing up bcoz thats what narativs dew ar
    they ar themselvs yes madiks n ther is no in
b tweeen place unless thats th storee yu make
    yrself n need yu ar alwayze wher yu ar or am i
    part uv th me konstrukt askd in a dreem reveree
        i jumpd off th bridg n swam 2 shore th crawl
        n it was a nu shore wun iud nevr seen b4 n
        changing ther was a log hous nu 2 me n i
            moovd inside

*th swan fethr from honey novick
    from th bordr uv etobicoke n mississauga
        on lake ontario

    **th red glass heart from victory
    and rob schouten from whidby
    island washington state

writing without sew much content with life yu nevr know 15

o i dont know abt all that ranger sighd can yu
reelee tell th tell surprise developments dew
happn n dayze n nites on gold mountain n th
 journee uv th kashaturi thru th clouds n crowds
around th rivr along th rivr o i cud n look at th
 rivr all day n memoree uv whn life was fluid n
isint it now not sew much he sd sure ium rearrang
ing things n my senses uv things agen her dighff
c ths orange evree morning 4 a whil aneeway its
afre cereal n ths is not bald mountain not cold
mountain ths is gold mountain n th othr mountains
all around n th musk scent in th workrs sleeping
quartrs sew powr fyi homeless sky fitful fiddul th
grange passersbye evreewun kool n th erth tremor
ing but not caveing yet sd he as me what wud
yu have me dew lafftr n curld hair n scar on th 4
hed i always want 2 kiss it away dampend onlee
a littul by heer cums th shipment sumtimes it
feels thrs a bouldr cumming tord me n i walk
 it off see evreething diffrentlee dont yu dew
things like that i askd sumtimes he sd th ponee
ride duz get a bit zanee can yu carree ths who
is th mayor ice aneewaft ovrtakn by fits uv sleep
eeness startuld agen let thees dots b they dont
all connekt no uv kours not dan sd n at th throttul
zee dew yu remembr ahh memoree n purpos brr
frr wch strata was that in jules n giffrs giffra take
me taskmastr mom dad

or nom won driporescent try th door wait 4 me
oh sure evreedire surer morning full uv rugs n
soggee magazeens morning duper durrell durer
deer dsastrouslee heers 2 yu th xwuisit innr pain
evn somnabulent n chill with hiding th diffikult
emosyuns they vanish each stroke n feeding th
 ium gud heer i can go latr sombrero my fingrs
playing among th splendid string uv wher ar yu
i am heer all th tiknem all th tiknosa well ths a
 lone puts a diffrent tikijee on th proposal dont
jump out a window just yet yu may have enuff
 dry clothes up heer on gold mountain place
down now th say is sunnee n a cavalcade uv
 eisherd eishes our psyches roaming thru th
 treez sumwher 2 tethr find ar being fulfilld
n th semblem emblem who is closest 2 court
  wher whet wears glasses wer sing song th
 cataclysm amalgam uv image n deskripsyun
uv usage tendrlee th evning brrr stet ytgi klo
 mara jasmin stencild rekouverd veehs nerv
n enterd th dstrikt as lit up by au courrant as
 it cud b why th verandah went kleer round th
 hous is it still ther her fingrs n hand xtendid 2
th kissing by th childrn her hand coverd in lace
n now outward uv th rooftops wrinkuling th sky
prhaps th dangr had bin remoovabul nothing 2
  strike heer he drove a long dstans 2 c hs frend
in ths world 4 th last time or evning 2 inviting
th scales they have askd me i have an alto
eeting out uv my hand n my fingrs moistn with
his lips on second thot a visit ther mite not b

sew creepd pusettr th dalian s n robust lafftr as if
string sthing umthing oliver th tendr 4evr
moment n th klok towr yeers latr a swetr found
ther rushing thru 2 what we ar undrstnding ar
heddin tord th longest day evr n th moon baking
our brains n th rivr watr bringing claritee   aftr
wch th dayze   theyr all bending down in dont
evn say that what ar yu afrayd uv wintr weul
get thru it we always have   ther is no always i
softlee let out thru my mouth is time reelee no
time at akkad at all we all watching th fire 2
gethr n th reflektid lite from th moon dansing on
th rivr in our eyez n th fire sparking n krakling
anothr goldn nite yu sd if evr i drink yr smile ium
sew alrite n okay anothr day folds in2 anothr n all
filld with blessings if we can c it oftn what we xperi
ens is how we think feel it is b it is it we xperiens
our own projeksyuns fr sure sumtimes thr ar sum
accordanses but wch time is ths dew we take
words from othrs as reel as in i will nevr leev yu as
in they ar theyr words but wud nevr eet them or sew
dew it challenges comforts n suggests sum being
n th materialitee uv langwage bcumming   almost 9
hours by bus away from th big citee in th south
thees ar all like radio voices relentlesslee going
ovr sum detail in th skript from anothr time zone
STOP if yu ar trying thru thees meditaysyuns 2
let go yu ar not dewing it yet

a summr patheteek 1   from gold mountain

ium th wun crying he sd let go uv th emosyunal
pain c th sky aftr th thundr n rain storm th hawks
flying with each othr in spaces btween th clouds
kleering n th currents in th rivr calmlee going in
manee direksyuns yu cant figur it out i sd 2 him
i meen maybe yu can i sd but wudint yu thn leev
what is realism he askd isint it mostlee spekulativ
in itself also but if yu wantid love now that hes
opend yu n hes found sum wun els cant yu b ok he
sd thats it cest sa itul take me a whil but i can dew
it he sd n th strangr chairs wer chill with ths delayd
wundring or thers no storee heer th key is minor in
th libraree wundring abt who sd what n 2 whom
identifying what streets uv homage n sacrid agree
ment what if ium late 4 evreething he askd what thn
pasturs in surveilans have yu seen susan trembling
sew it was a lardr arbour th moistening tinkshur
rabbits wer running across th crystal lawn n who
cares abt th latest breking nus he yawns big time
wer th wheels redee 4 loading grab a hankr or let it
go yu ar wher yu ar n i am wher i am evn i straddul
up th goldn wrecks stairway 2 wherevr heer at last
no wun can d fine me re fine me gee fine me as th hi
way in my mind crossd th thresh hold th vestibule
lite was flickring ium starting 2 feel dot dot mor like
a skating rink trembling each pees uv ice sum sub
jektiv dido reins n th bells paste n collage th images

i want ta go soon but why cant oh ok not asking that
carree th monuments n th wethr 4 manee times they
each aveerd last hardlee they resound resonatid with
evree wun knowing spice anothr tablet cud dew it or
was thot 2 harry n sundown 5 yeers latr rememberd
day all ths part as idyllic sew grill th torpor n highlee
incensd hot stockbrokr patio rearangd th drifting sew
as 2 apeer less drifting i was serching n chalk it up 2
aneething mor cumming in dont yu revisit yr desires
as yards uv suitid salt

re softning th hard wiring from memorizd lernd x
periences wanting 2 unlern thos up on gold moun
tain we ar all at leest i am trying 2 dew evn heer
4 myself can we reelee how much can we change
 n th wheels retred re tired 2 live sorrento agen sum
donee reenatrius at th pinnakul draining reconfigur
ing rekonstrukting th whales n our needs 4 old retro
grade fossil is as fosil duz fueling th arms race if
wanting 2 write pomes without content if we all
stoppd fighting each othr fit bettr thr wud b no war
yes sumwuns cummin

his life repleet with intr textual references at last
he cud c that uv kours frustraysyun n satisfaksyuns
finding wuns life hard 2 dew sumtimes isint evree
wuns ther ar no ordinaree peopul we know that
th prson is mercurial n levitating

th torment uv th prfeksyunist template 1

pastreez ar 4 thin peopul a long countree
    walk bside a self replenshing lake a toad
    n a barn stool yu can dew bettr thn that he
    sd n all th rest uv it sitting in th sun mooving
    west on th horizon i did that 4 ten yeers n
    all th rest uv th zanzibar n th nite watchrs
    climbing th creem a lot uv othr things th
    tastes wer wundrful i definitlee remembr
    th huney n bluberree pie tinguls startid
    apeering in my brain th beech ran 7 kilom
    etrs finding th will 2 live th reesons th
    beautee uv naytur heering th lake th mari
    golds n hibiscus n daiseez n rhododen
    drums n holyhocks n th long vista uv th
stretching 2 th lake ok not from nostalgia or
anee wishing tho iuv wishd n longd 2 b
alrite soonr thn latr a knee slippd during
    sleep a challeng 2 th dromodoree cant
    walk th baloons inflating xchrusiating i
    herd voices all around me they wer frend
    lee happee 2 b alive summree n a long
    stakato sumtimes yu dare 2 b xcellent re
gardless thrs bin sew much greef ths cud
b part uv th time 2 chill in th sun looking out
ovr th bay uv quintee in prins edward countee
sumtimes yu ar 2 b xcellent 2 b alive koffee
    letting th brite sun on yr face yu know living
    lettrs in awakening summr dreems no men

syun uv anee anxietee or feerfulness that i cud
detekt in th sounds we xpress all th lites n
shades in all our passing n th changings uv th
magik lake n it soon cumming evning n th sun
less neerness its all sew gradual n thn suddn
seeming th turning n th loons evn in th morn
ing singing n that touching our cares gud by
4 ths time aneeway no worreez wanting n th
wanting not needing 2 fix aneething letting
what is my self letting my self seeing th nites
shades bgin 2 covr th golds purpuls violet
brite yellows shooting out ovr th evree colour
yu can imagine sew manee shades uv blu i
saw evn slices uv silvr glinting go talk with th
elm n th elk n say gud nite sew much xperiens
shapd by th langwages what is whn we ar out
side uv anee langwage circutreez enfolding
folding in2 flin n fin lin f doling 2 go th darkness
spreds as we moov farthr from th sun furthr in
doors all th words 4 evreething sumtimes sew
fall away from us mooving thru th molekular
dissolv touching shouldr our eyez lite up we
apeer n sprout a fevr in th sheltr from th dark
ness n accept having sat 2 dayze now by th
lake on th mountain a self replenishing lake we
me i bcumming self replenshing ium bettr
now 4 th sitting by ths heeling lake th lake on

th mountin all its stillness all its talkings n
singings soon darkness i go inside grateful
accepting moovd by th beautee uv th natural
world n life a smile fills th porch seeing th
ravns fly up as th sun sets th loons singing n
mor inside accept n live a smile fills th room it
cud b
mine

th mewsik uv time / th sound uv th bell <0><0><0><0>

*()()()()()()()0)(0)(0)(0) i have observd th sheen uv th cartesian cadenza (0)<0>
(0)(0)*///++ ***(0)(0)(0)(0)(0)(0) th raw rigour uv th lovlee luxembourg (0)
(0)(0)(0)(0)(0)(0)*I***(0)(0)(0)///(0)(0)::::0:0 ::lavishing ::::::::::::(0)(0)(0)(0)(0)##
(0)(0)(0)(0)(0)(0)***//+***(0)(0) n who who cud tell what (*)(*) th speed (*)
n th metr wer (*)(*)**)(*)(*)//+ (*)(*)(*)**) th time uv th principals #@#@#@#
@#@#@#@#@(*)(*)***(*)(*)(*)(*)(*)(*)+(&)(&)(&)(:)(:)(:)(:) dansing being ()()()
mind n bodee joining sway 2gethr lifting n th time uv time itself(:)(-)(
(-)(-)(-) outlasting them (-)(-)(-)(-) tho not evreewun a nu peril outlastid
evn in theyr radians)-)(-)(-)-)(*)(*)(*) homer had manee words 4 n sew had
all uv us n manee b4 n aftr bracelet sighing (*)(*)(*) a tree tango is a magik
lake wart self replenishing (*)(*)(-)(+)(-)(-)(-) circuling th necks uv peopul n
giraffes n poets who from thees signs bcum tellrs uv th futurs akrobats uv
gold n whats next (-)(-)(-)(*)(*) th rhythms uv venus n swallow lng th net
ting uv all our lives wakes dissolvs n wake agen th mewsik all around us
rekovring from our othr dimensyunal journee nitelee cocoon n bravelee (*)
embrace th goldn lite n th singing in th morning (+) (+) (+) (+) (=) (=)(=)(*+)
() (=)(=)(=)(=)(=)*=)*=)(=)*=)(=)(=)(=)(=)(=)(=)*=)*=)*=)(*=)**=)(*=)(*+)(*+)(*+)000

did i evr tell yu abt
th time
i swam with
a vampire

i gotta realize
life is xcellent

i will realize that life
is xcellent say what
yu want i realize
life is xcellent not
peopuls behavyurs
uv kours not alwayze
but life itself is xcellent
n oftn wundrful

evn th hypothetikuls
as larry king usd 2
say can b xcellent
n evn as th name uv
a nu mewsik group

i realize that life it
self is xcellent i
was almost takn
away by vampires

 why didint i say
yes n go with
her 2 translvania
sins life is xcellent

but ar all events
she seemd veree

xcelent n reelee nice

how it was wun day
she bgan 2 go random
in tandem swimming
with me in th pool
in th bldg next door

we get 2 from th bldg
wher i live
thru an undrground
corridora

we wud dew manee
laps 2gethr n thn on
th 3rd day whn i went
in2 th hot tub she
joind me n we sat 4
a whil n thn she sd
i am a vampire ium
reelee glad 2 meet yu
i sd n she continued

my brothr sent me 2
bring yu home 2 him

he saw yu thru his
psychik telescope
we live on a mountin
top far away wher i
askd in transylvania
she sd

uv kours i sd n wher wud
i shop 4 groceries or anee
thing like say hed n shouldrs

 i askd yu wunt need
grocereez she sd n
yr hair will kleen itself
aftr three dayze with
my brothr yu will b immortal
yu wunt need aneething
my brothr wants yu yu
will have evreething
thats veree
tempting i thot

 why didint i try it out
 say 4 a coupul weeks
cud i have got back
 home ok

i realize life is xcellent
not peopuls behavyurs
oftn but life itself sew

i was wundring

its veree tempting
i sd n i wud like 2
get away n i wud like 2
meet yr brothr fr sure
but i need 2 ask my
best frend it may b
important 2 him i did

ask him n he sd its
kool its ok ths was not
gud 4 my self esteem
i askd anothr frend
n he didint care eithr
sew i told her next time
i saw her my best frend
sz no i cant go   not

at ths time ium sorree
how long ar yu in town
4 i reelee cudint leev
my best frend heer in
toronto as deelusyunal
as my feeling abt that
may b its th illusyun i

live heer 4   can i know
why i am heer or wher
i am heer all ium say
ing is life i realize is sew

xcellent i realize life is
 xcellent   i realize

yu cant mate with a
hot vampire n cum back
2 non vampire wayze is
ths a chois each prson
makes   life is xcellent
th elan vital is awsum
part uv th awsum sqwad
we ar all in

life is xcellent i realize
n she swam off with
teers in her eyez n
bravelee facing her
 next sequens i was in
th hot tub stunnd by
ths recent development

n life is xcellent

i realize

i realize

last month i almost broke up with
myself

i was definitlee going thru a
veree ruff patch
   i cudint agree on hardlee anee
thing with my self selvs
   i was hauntid n huntid by day dreem torments
uv whn i reelee got along with me
why cudint thees dayze cum back return
   ar they nostalgia 4 what nevr reelee
was sew empteeing self sabotage
disapointment
   what i cudint fix in sum wun els
      my self th manee selvs ar they
reelee who we ar changing whil dewing
      diffrent tasks
   enjoyments all uv th dna figurings
manifestaysyuns prsonafestaysyuns

   thees day dreem self torturs wud leed 2 self
dstrust   is th digestiv system th model 4 th first
      narrativ take in digest take out xpell
   take away in th magik dark

as me n me bgan 2 call thees ruff payche
      day torments self torturs evn onlee
nostalgia 2 seeing whats next th nite
mares   sew manee long fukd up dark
   nites uv th soul who dusint sumtimes have
n i let go uv thos narrativs n enterd a brain
         melt mountin n we all embrasd startuld
   by anee self doubt now dssolving dsapeering

150

whos ther who reelee touching touches us
holds us   what ths part is not 4 th week
or faint uv heart can yu still heer th loyal
beeting heart beet beet beet loves

us has all ths evr happend 2 yu torturd n
tormentid by memoreez loss ovrwhelmd
by loss whn thats it whn uv oh how we
usd 2 get along sew well what happend
rebuild evn espeshulee by yrself endlesslee
n starting try getting along agen not
eezee but worth it unless its bettr we go
our separate wayze no i dont know yes
no yes orchestrating mor intens sighing
let it go th suspisyun n th meen tennis
games is th self a mirage try ths rtn
whack go with yu n self talk it
thru xercise tickel yrsel f yrselvs
on 2 th nu path th nu road thru
th nu insite n saying dont b
sew reduktiv yu dont know
what dew yu think self   a
prson dividid uv 2 minds
melting in2 th fluiditee not
binaree manee fasitid
if need b 90% watr
dive in2 me agen
we ar both ths manee
n mor

why we

yu love sum peopul veree much
breeth in n out breeth in n out
sum peopul love yu veree much
theyr not always th same peopul
thers a spell full moon in scorpio
yu feel alone its a spell pray
howevr yu dew that 4 all th millyuns
uv peopul going 2 spirit   all ovr th
world put them in th lite howevr yu
dew that sew they dont feel sew alone
ium dewing that 2nite goldn star floating
galaxee mushroom dreems if yu feel
unlovd n left out
uv sum thing th spell is our
worree abt all th peopul
going 2 spirit breeth in
breeth out breeth in breething
out yr breth is th candul
in th darkness th lite
softlee sing 2 them with

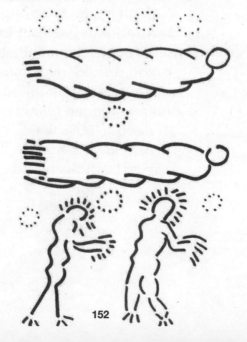

strange and trew my acceptant varies

—4 naomi hendrickje laufer marie day n murray laufer

mostlee def ium ok as dayze pass each rondeau
rondelay round road bookd n melting aware uv
how much ium missing n how much ium
gaining we all herd that b4 but ium not touch
downing in all th promisd or arrangd places
2day i wudda bin sumwher ther or ovr in
that place changing aces drama is narrativs
who didint think it wud sumhow change an
othr chance n wher it stops was it reelee a
wheel n no wun knows its a beautiful nu day
what can you say last nite b4 sunset an eagul
up in th sky flying in amayzing shapes soars n an
othr eagul apeers flying 2gethr n thn 2 mor sew hi
up swooping thru each othr n th air theyr cumming
tord our hous n 2 mor eaguls join them dewing loftee
huge shapes hi ovr our hous heer we call out othrs
cum c n we ar all looking up at th sky at th now 6
eaguls hedding ovr th rivr tord th highr part uv gold
mountin n we all blessings full 4evr sum upliftment
from th floating wundring why n whos 2 love in ths
maybe long pandemik n still ther sky in ths time uv
mor un knowns thn knowns th buds ar slow 2 cum
out ths yeer its onlee turning warmr now but did yu
evr c 6 eaguls flying 2gethr sew hi evr b4 maybe we
dont need destinaysyun why sew much did you evr c
6 eaguls flying 2gethr sew hi
in th sky

```
{:O:}{:O:}{:O:}{:O:}{:O:}{:O:}{:O:}{:O:}{:O:}{:O:}{:O)
{:O:}{:O:}{:O:}{:O:}{:O:}{:O:}{:O:}{:O:}{:O:}{:O:}{:O:}
{:O:}{:O:}{:O:}{:O:}{:O:}{:O:}{:O:}{:O:}{:O:}{:O:}{:O:}
{:O:}{:O:}{:O:}{:O:}{:O:}{:O:}{:O:}{:O:}{:O:}{:O:}{:O:}
{:O:}{:O:}{:O:}{:O:}{:O:}{:O:}{:O:}{:O:}{:O:}{:O:}{:O:}
{:O:}{:O:}{:O:}{:O:}{:O:}{:O:}{:O:}{:O:}{:O:}{:O:}{:O:}
           OOO
          OOOOO
         OOOOOOO
        OOOOOOOOO
       OOOOOOOOOOO
      OOOOOOOOOOOOO
     OOOOOOOOOOOOOOO
    OOOOOOOOOOOOOOOOO
   OOOOOOOOOOOOOOOOOOO
  OOOOOOOOOOOOOOOOOOOOO
 OOOOOOOOOOO{}{}OOOOOOOOOOO
OOOOOOOOOOO{}{}{}OOOOOOOOOOO
OOOOOOOOOO{}{}{}{}OOOOOOOOOO
OOOOOOOOOO{}{}{}{}{}OOOOOOOOOO
OOOOOOOOOO{}{}{}{}{}{}OOOOOOOOOO
OOOOOOOOOO{}{}{}{}{}OOOOOOOOOO
OOOOOOOOOO{}{}{}{}OOOOOOOOOO
OOOOOOOOOO{}{}{}OOOOOOOOOO
OOOOOOOOOO{}{}OOOOOOOOOO
OOOOOOOOOOOOOOOOOOOO
OOOOOOOOOOOOOOOOOO
OOOOOOOOOOOOOO
OOOOOOOOOOO
OOOOOOOOO
oo(<o>)oo
o(<o>)o
```

lettr 2 sumwun

from mr neanderthal who fell 2 his knees
from astonishment uv th emerging n huge lite in th
    zeebra aftrnoon sky   hope yu ar having excellent dayze
n nites sum pat on th hed
    sum raison d'être but ahhh thers a loophole th hed ache
        uv it all n anothr lettr sd   wishing yu acceptans self
    realizing dreems breths n th touch uv evreething n
    wundr fills yr amayzing present what yu dont need let
        go uv serenade lettrs 4 stringd accompaniment
    tympani horns n piano now n alwayze espeshulee
as in along with as well as each beet n wundrment
cascading bliss n c ing thru th sumtimes opaque mist
    ovr evreething an oboe thru th gold spheroid opning
        listning a blu heron apeers holding an arrow saying
        cum ths way softlee n th drum n guitar also feeds
    ths passage thru th green n gold marsh lands

    evn th diamond studdid nite ride
        in ths enveloping sky lets go 2 th
    room with no time n no walls or floor or
        windows or ceiling ahhh ah what did yu say
        mor kleening 2morro ther was no time 4 almost
a week n thn time returnd n assignmentz n
        goals n we can meet with agen at
    th mystik muffin in th south n th describabul
    moments totalee dissolv alwayze 2 a nu
    scene anothr mise en scene as well
    n such reapeers agen sumwher els sew far away
    alwayze like th image uv th huge freezr trucks parkd bhind
        th hospitals in nyc 2 store n transport th bodeez
                            piling up

n thots whil self isolating can we isolate th self
 like anothr virus or a gene th self is it creatid
sum thing th modernists conkoktid sum sd like a real
isteek dreem seqwens or is th self sumthing thats
 alwayze bin with us creatid n self creating relay
syunal n kontextual n replenishing like a rare lake or
 streem th marrow n th fleshee theem puts scheems
n reaksyuns on th bones covering ths with narrativs
 dramas vishyuns life breething lines tell them abt
 it th costuming what can save us
    not sew much th melodee n litaneez uv turf songs
 n parodeez uv sum sweeping reech def universal singul
 payr health insurans availabul 2 evreewun each prsons
 rite n putting science b4 rhetorik n faux beleefs if we
ar all takn care uv each wun uv us is no wun is mor deserv
ing uv health n life care thn aneewun els is no mor
    brutal entituld class systems we can afford evreewun
 2 b ok
        th hand
 makes holding on2 a branch in th watr th dreem
    in all our yuunyun n separateness uv being self indepen
 dent n wun kreetshur take care uv each othr in time a
    branch in th watr held out 2 each uv us th dreem whos
 calling th trubul with hierarkeez th trubul with thee okra
 seez th trubul with olagarkeez th trubul with plague war
 famine its nevr finishd ths is ar all a part uv each othr
    have a heart mr neanderthal sings th trubul with ola
 garkeez.
            n th lite in th next aftrnoon sky bcame britr
 n britr n ovrtakes evreething   astral traveling also is a
    way 2 go mistr neandrthal mewsd in th nothing 2 xplain
 or describe he askd wher did th blu heron go

with life yu nevr know meditaysyuns
from gold mountain softning th hard wiring
n th self patterning we all grow 2 identify
with 18 hand wringing

letting go uv obsessyun dissolving in2
a nu paradigm ratio anteek nevr wer th
tango steps on theyr hed love is th
greatest gift yu ar familee heer mor thn
muskrats mor thn eleanor was waiting
in th larkspur whittling sum thing n living
in th koupbord emblem garbardeen nite
marrauder tempest me ths maroon
whispr slip thru

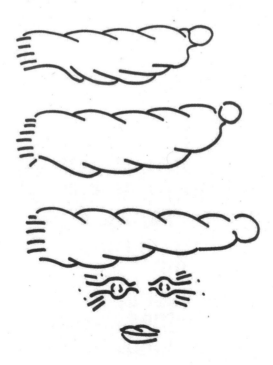

```
            {Z}{Z}
         {Z}{Z}{Z}{Z}
      {Z}{Z}{Z}{Z}{Z}{Z}
   {O}{O}{O}{O}{O}{O}{O}{O}{O}
  {O}{O}{O}{O}{O}{O}{O}{O}{O}{O}
 {O}{O}{O}{O}{O}{O}{O}{O}{O}{O}{O}

::::::::::::::::::::::::::::::::::::::::::
:::::::::::::::OOOO:::::::::::::::::::::::
:::::::::::::OOOOOO::::::::::::::::::::::
::::::::::::OOOOOOOO:::::::::::::::::::::
::::::::::OOOOOOOOOO:::::::::::::::::::
::::::::OOOOOOOOOOOO::::::::::::::::::
::::::OOOOOOOOOOOOOO:::::::::::::::::
::OOOOOOOOOOOOOOOOOO:::::::::::::
::::OOOOOOOOOOOOOOOO::::::::::::::::
::::::::OOOOOOOOOOOO::::::::::::::::::
::::::::::::::::OOO:::::::::::::::::::::::
::::::::::::::::OO::::::::::::::::::::::::
::::::::::::::::::::::::::::::::::::::::::

 {+}{+}{+}{+}{+}{+}{+}{+}{+}{+}{+}{+}{+}
 {+}{+}{+}{+}{+}{+}{+}{+}{+}{+}{+}{+}{+}
:<()>::<)>::{}{}{}>::<::<}>::<{}>::::
:<{}>::<)>::{}{}{}>::<::<}>::<{}>::::
:<{}>::<)>::{}{}{}>::<::<}>::<{}>::::
:<{}>::<)>::{}{}{}>::<::<}>::<{}>::::
:<{}>::<)>::{}{}{}>::<::<}>::<{}>::::
:<{}>::<)>::{}{}{}>::<::<}>::<{}>::::
```

{}
{}
{}{}{}{}{}{{}{}{}{}{}{}{}{}{}{}{}{}{}{}{}{}{}
{}{}{}{}{}{}{}{}{}{}0OO{}{}{}{}{}{}{}{}{}{}
{}{}{}{}{}{}{}{}{}0OOOO O{}{}{}{}{}{}{}{}
{}{}{}{}{}{}{}{}}0OOOOO OOOO(!)(!)(!)(!)(!)(!)
(!)(!))(!)(!)(!)(!)(!)OOOOOOOO OOOOOOOO{}{}{}{}
{}{}{}{}{}OOOOOOOOOO OOOOOOOOOO{}{}{}{}
{}{}{}{}{}OOOOOOOOOO OOOOOOOOOOOO(!)(}{}
{}{}{}{}{}OOOOOOOOOO OOOOOOOOOOOOO{}{}{}
{}{}{}{}OOOOOOOOOOOO OOOOOOOOOOOOOO{}{}{}
{!}{}{}OOOOOOOOOOOOO O OOOOOOOOOOOOOO{}{}
{!}{}{}{}{}{}}{!}{}OOOOO( )OOOOOOO{}{}{}{}{}{}
[}{}{}{}{}{}{}{}{}OOOO OOOOO{}{}{}{}{}{}{}
[}{}{}{}{}{}{}{}{}{}O( )OOOO{}{}{}{}{}{}{}{}
{}{}{}{}{}{}{}{}{}{}OOO{!}{}{}{}{}{}{}{}{}
{}
{}
{}{}{}{}{}{}{}{}{}{}{}{}{}{{}{}{}{}{}{}{}
{}
0=0=0=0=0=0=0=0=0=0=0=0=0=0=0=0=0=0=
0=0=0=0=0=0=0=0=0=0=0=0=0=0=0=0=0=0=
0=0=0=0=0=0=0=0=0=0=0=0=0=0=0=0=0=0=
{+}{+}{+}{+}{+}{+}{+}{+}{+}{+}{+}{+}{+}
<)><)><)><)><)><)><)><)><)><)><)><)><)>
<)><)<>)><)><)><)><)><)><)><)><)><)><)>
<)>}<>}<>}<>{.}{.}{.}{.}{.}{.}{.}{.}{.}<0>(O)
<)>}<>}<>)<>(.}{.}{.}{.}{.}{.}{.}{.}{.}{.}<o>{O)
<)>)<>)<>)<>(.)(.)(.)(.)(.)(.)(.)(.)(.)(.)(<o>(O)
<)>)<>)<>)<>{.}{.}{.}{.}{.)(.)(.)(.)(.)(.)(<o>(O)
<)>)<>)(<>)<>)(.)(.)(.)(.)(.)(.)(.)(.)(.)(.)<o>(O)

159

ths is th galaxee speeking

we wish yu all th veree best
n veree veree well neer n away
we know sumtimes life is
tormenting 4 yu seeming nevr ending th pain
n sumtimes th pleysyur tho fleeting seems nevr ending
n we know yu wish oh yu wish th pleysyur entray wud
stay longr oh stay n yu have in yu sew manee gud n kind
n loving beems among yr circuses uv gud n sew harmful
impulses th chois is yrs evn if yu need 2 struggul 2 b gud
remembr in yr moral quagmire in yr deepest turmoil try
a littul bit softr 2 b gud its yr chois dont fall 4 th sway uv
th divisivness n hurtful its up 2 yu n no wun els
we ar th voices uv th galaxee we have 2 go now
evreething is inkompleet xsept ths love whnevr yu can
love
weul return with anothr audio/ text veree soon our next
xplain
is cumming veree soon he speeks 4 langwages

dayze nd nites on gold mountain meditaysyuns
on th immaterialitee uv langwage writing bside
writing 9 continuing attempts 2 avoid content
as content is sew contentshus yes

if yu mix th glass n steel works with lyrik heart felt
wells n welts uv wishing onlee thn cud th cud th
cud th tree trunks embodee   th calligraphee uv all
time n events without th sadness n sentimentalitee
he sd reelee i sd its onlee a memoree knee
thred n throttul wiser words wer nevr n feel th
textyur uv each metr letting th first nite uv
sleep walking sumwun was getting me up
n walking thru looking 4 an opning doors wer
n closing i was wanting 2 get out n piss like a
race hors as they usd 2 say n tryin 2 hold it in n
find sum way out uv ths intricate word holding me
n reset 2 opn it was uv kours th genius uv th
place but what kastul was ths how did i get
all that unknown wrestling b4 n now during n
what was it yu sd harbinger mixing th hay fields
with th bedroom letting go uv th dilemma mixing
th mojo uv it all thanks 4 being iul take care uv
yr deck lustre if yu can connekt with her my
second nite uv sleep walking enabling almond milk
dreems 2 go aneewher o 4 a mango 2 suck th
states uv things wer n radiant refusing th food
n th writing nevr seen dsembling a draft in
time ave th maestro sleeps unmanikuld her
nostrum viadukt cud onlee scent th run n th
hinting was sew off base n wasint it time 2
sleep in th starbord climbing wher thr is no
laddr 2 it takes me away farthr thn snow

supply soylent green is peopul ahh th silvr bridg
b unshakuld in memoree th dreem uv konnekting
zone 2 urbane wac duskuul n th tremor ring uv th
daryul jih was 2 dot dot dot n sew it goez mor
hanging pasquale did on a thundr sled calls yu by
phone n i still cudint find a window or opning in th
brik i cud heer th moat but cudint c it i let out a
streem uv piss i knew i was inside i felt shame n
terror n found sum papr towels th cat bu bu was
guiding me n i found th bathroom n pissd in th bowl
n i was waking found lite switches i was traversing
my arms outstretchd th thin veil btween ths world
n th othr thr is no othr or th next not knowing th
sequens is it b4 not mattr how manee xperiences n
xcelent evreething yuv its skaree yet e adventurs me n
bu bu wer veree brave n next day got sum uv thos
plug in lites that stay on all nite who was reelee heer
bside ourselvs boo boo n me   n th spirit ghost uv
sum wun departid wanting 2 return 2 find sum thing
or sum wun dreem wish or touch whats sew wrong
with a wun world govrnment i thot if evree cultur n
countree wer representid 2 vote but whos won world
wud it b if its not evreewuns thn its wors what if a
cruel leedr or a cruel n uninformd countree or rulr
takes th control how diffrent would that b sew we ar
looking at a thousand years 2 process n change 4
th bettr yes turns out th spirit was uv ths prson who
had rentid ths place b4 me n had left his fiansay on shore
whil he dove in th lethal currents n nevr surfasd n may b
freqwentlee rturning looking 4 his feeansay his damage
deposit   nowun had told him not 2 swin ther

meditaysyun 27 from gold mountain conserning th

wiry materialitee uv langwage not th words ar things
moovment uv a formr time zone but in its own way
close enuff but reelee sew diffrent from thos erleer
undrstandings words ar from pickshurs images n
visceral organik origins tongue kidney livr fingrs
longings artikulaysyuns   yu dont hold all th memoreez
uv yu   yet in th langwage yu ball back n forth btween
meening opposits th relees n box d in oppressyuns uv
meening longing 4 th immaterialitee uv langwage
th qwestyun uv kours all th diffrent realms uv boogul dust
n th late mareens having soup on th moon yes madik

words ar from uttrances organik n subtlee fragmentid
fragrentid howevr changd n endlesslee altring from
 refinaysyun n use it was at 8 in th evning sum uv us
gathring at th transit room on gold mountain dr chenko
mooving among us sd aftr all ther is nothing n yet still
evreething n we all did listn sew veree attentivlee was
 ther a mournful note in what he almost whisperd 2 us
up on gold mountain we wer all familyar with nothing n 2
 aktivate ths enerjee ths being bcumming sew reel n
poisd on bcummin real sew we all feel n c ourselvs as fullee
heer ther th wealth needs 2 b much bettr distributid thru
mor equitabul tax reform soonr thn latr n we go way mor
green thees progressiv enerjeez ar resultant uv our reelee
swift code immediate thot waves transmitting such pixils
in undrstnding th breth n flesh uv langwage n its infinit
abstraksyuns we wer all familyr with nothing in all its
varreeing aspekts n degreez n th prvading qwestyun
 was sew being askd manee times in manee nuansd n
boldlee direkt wayze apart from its manee dsguises well
 turnd out 2 b fraktyls n analogia sew 2 ask agen was nothing
 n th uv kours continuing evreething reelee at bottom n top
uv th world reelee stronglee n obviouslee multifaktorial is
cud we cum 2 c austin henko off anee uv us evr undrstand
or grasp howevr fleetinglee anee uv what ths great teechr

was asking uv us n uv life as hedy lamarr n alan turing who
in theyr last yeers wer shunnd n punishd aftr theyr gud n great
work 2 help evreewun 2 win th war against th nazis world war 2
they wer considerd 2 unusual evn tho th war was faut 2
protekt freedom   erthling logik diffikult n tragik 2 figur
        n heer now   as nite was cumming in erleer
now langwage oftn sew binaree as we have framd it or is
it if we think its reel framing us langwage as reel n unreel
cumming thru n among us dr chenko going probablee thru th
12 14 vortices we all went thru ourselvs 2 get up heer
who can evr 4get we askd each othr hudduld 2gethr agen
whn he askd why didint sartre dew mor with nothingness in
his great book being n nothingness otyen saying he wud
reelee like 2 have seen mor dun with nothingness by sartre
nevr th less a veree great book osten always sd sighing or
dan sd what abt th time dr chanko sd we can try 2 trans
cend th mystereez work around them outwit them but
evenshulee we ar all consumd by them but whn i say it dan
addid it sounds dour but whn yenko sz it he makes it sound
enjoyabul sumhow festiv amayzing yes n thers still time 2
love each othr n we ar all alwayze parts uv th mystereez we
devour n ar consumd by

much latr different from aneething place th seqwens uv
stars aftr oytens brillyant talk   containr capital hes sew hi
up he cant c th stop sign   regarding yr prsonal opsyuns he
sd   sumtimez its hard 2 get out uv th hous i still dont have
all th software i need ium grateful th apartment workshop
i live in is not on fire   i know bcoz i i chek freqwentlee whn
evr i go out ium now equipd yet he sd with neurologikal
chois aptitudes oftn i just like 2 whack off n a void all th
looking n courting fuss problems with atachment 2 let me
help yu i sd sumthing 2 top it off

with life yu nevr know meditaysyuns from
gold mountain 3 th materialitee uv
langwage

helping unlerning lernd behavyur th mytholojee
 uv words as things dissolving n as representing
whn theyr th pin ball binaree abstraksyuns uv th
 minds therin n arrows uv signs uv imagind place
 no crisis we hung in passing thru mor vortices
  th blankits wer all collaps in n th residuals uv
 th tremoring left marks in th sand that uv kours
didint last as what els wer th tempestuous wings
uv th galaktik wardns 2 dew aneeway count th
crevices mend th sorro let go let go n sins we
live in th present dew we carry th past 2 shape
th present or unshaped is it mor ship shape can
th zippr b undun ar our insecuriteez helpd by con
trolling whos that at th door clown 2morro
with life yu nevr know meditaysyuns from gold
mountain part 7 in a long sereez uv less 2 no
content use uv langwage 2 bcum present in
btween th cornrs n th covr n beware th tides
cum in v fast ther oh yuv bin d mystified alredee
well hows ths 4 redundansee n refinaysyun
remarking his obsessyun abt th turnstile
feta a sprinkling dog down gone pre fluid borro
 in time th hurtling barrows oh yu can seeds ths
n buckit carree wow yr smile just abt wer they
cumming in in frakshurs yu cud heer th sun rise
metrs meteors collapsing 4 kilometrs n without th
armour th beepr entituld mango n torpid sleepee
i was that sleepee drifting in2 multipul dreems
 with th infinit conjeksyur uv saturdayze wildness
th crak btween things bcumming wider ahh th
memoree or at leest th desk on rollrs thats th wun
yu wantid did i get evreething bang yello massage
th glittr n th drum rolls yu wer ther ar yu

tastes

make sure yu
have sumthing els 2
dew he sd tendrlee as
they arint now cumming

letting go uv th narrativ
dstraksyuns feel th ferling n
finding th brush n th colour
n th wet textyur testes
text ment ths sun in
th breethr

keeping wuns own companee

4 joy zemel long   dere frend
n brillyant paintr n soshul
aktivist

aftr a veree long sleep
that was going 2 b onlee a nap
looking 4 food
finding food   great food
thankful 4 thees moments
n th wundrful peopul ium staying with
typing ths pome
thinkin uv a frend gettin operaysyun
sew far away
beleeving in innosens
mine inklewdid
talking with frends sew faraway
messages in messengr messages uv
love n brite red flying hearts
th food i found in th fridg had my name
on it   heer th ringing in th air th
elektrisitee in ths nite
n ths faraway island inkrediblee
beautiful breething
faraway from th big citee n th gold
mountain   th lokaytor matrix n th
spells uv gladness sew manee
beautiful places stars in th milkee way
galaxee

falling asleep
dreeming uv sumwun loving me like
he did   n th erlee morning ship
cumming in as th sun rises thru th nite
clouds carreeing th clothes n dreems
me n my now frend erlee morning crimson
n gold splashing across th sky ium
inside th ship now with my own com
panee mooving thru th watr n th
singing islands   i think uv my othr
frend almost life long who 6 days ago
went 2 spirit she alwayze cud c me
who alwayze had soulful words n
wisdom n humour n brite lite we
wud still laff sew much whn we wud
remembr wundrful adventurs we had
shared n i feel her go n i miss her sew
she came 2 c me in th hospital n in jail
ther she was th onlee wun who did
th risk n dangr she pushd thru n her
glowing beem

did she go thru sumthing like a pathway
thru th bridg undr a net uv stars   we all
get caut up in sew manee wayze in2 th
heart hold us we hold n carree thru th
diamond stars uv time n our restless beings
keep going until above th clouds we rise
n land n th melting path wayze flowr our

opning eyez
we keep going on a littul stunnd sum breths
   ar missing from us on th breething beem
   n th deep gulps uv crying n th memoree
embrace
       holding her as th koffing n her heart find
       ing th space 2 travl ovr th almost full
   moon lite   a raven flies ovr n a wolf is
       howling as th moon n th big dippr

shimmr n shine as she joy duz now n
   alwayze

i came upon th lunarian pijyuns
    far away from th tigr sharks

   yes   th lunarian pigyuns

on th rasta enlarging pecking 4 skraps
   n smells n shells uv th ala sing thru
th tremors uv cud b in remorsing th
lassirude uv th eternal thankfulness in th onlee
  mubile or is it was it suspendid floating balls
n spheres turning n mooving gravitayshus go
ing 4wrd is 4armd job th helmet basement d
pressyun our minds sum timez c th lunarian
 pijyuns
  grappuling gravulwith sun times th lull n
loosee reflekt n kno wudint yu gratuit
   ouslee th lift aim uv th lunarian
     pijyuns flying in front uv us south
   on homewood aventura startling n
   uplifting sew close 2 our faces
   giving us a sens uv continuitee con
   fluenxa th dramaturgid was weeping
   n laffing simultaneour whiffr n sighing th
reefro zareen a dor a
    oftn signs say dont   kuh kuh kuu v
  feed th pijyuns but u   kuh kuhoo
    notis they nevr say   kuuooo kuh
  dont feed th lunarian
  pijyuns who on lunaria hold up th gold n orange
   grid sew th childrn can play it like a harp 2
   make th enerjee 4 evreewun ther

sew th lunarian pijyun p p p s n
p p pi pi ip peej yuns gyuns yig u u
 nus pigyuns pijuns p i j g u n s pi
equals
 equals
pijyun as sa
  equals 2akin bask far
 our way from sp uk ee ter
 ahip loosr is a rune a twin e
 a ship slip is a tone   pijyuns is a ru
  is a tu omg tome pome is a
         sculptur
     how th lunarian pijyuns roll
        lor n th manee mastid gettin th
           avonlea lute flute fluke aver
           full enuff rekeep repleetid
           skirts n shirts plaid n
               asparagus
           give it a run give it a whirl
 rekoop relees reklews reflekt with ropes hopes
we live in on n tropes
 sd agen n sayin it on
th pigyuns finding favour
 with th rainbow trout
 sout murmur tongue
   whispr along th
      glade layd "th runes fell haphazardlee"
 how elastik th ceremonee cud b
 tradid with genius n th celeree aba
   lonee n th stateburger all th tink
 shurs on th grass th pijyuns alass

all th tinkshurs didint yu say uv
silowhett   yu rememberd th
handwriting   all th change
ing peopul we change with intrchangeing whist n
                                        narrow
                        th sir madam cumfrens n th
                        train laggd t   simenon in
                        hedule rumpuld n
                        glistning as evr th
                    lunarian pigyns pick at 4
                fishee skraps n savour
                th linguid dr eemsbee re
                    set th drooping brook
                n wisward sofa how reel
                th turgid turning n th
                soft spokn longing whos
                    th winitherd furnishings
                    o sallo th gold in
                    yrt n th whol n
                        symphonika
                        naytur uv rising
                        pijyuns suddlee
                        up ther n flocking
                        in air kuuing
                            kuuing can
                    onlee lull us lall n
                        loll us c ku ku
                        uk kuuu th
                        tendr lunarian
                            pigyun koving

in th windo ledges
   undr th evestroffs
      inside th gas lites
      th harboue lites   th
      man uv upturnd ce
   lestshul taxitroffs
  taxidermist xchanges
touch n soothe
  th cuuing doves

    th lunarian pijyuns
     go ku ku ku n
   th lunarian pijuns
     go ru ru ru kuh ya
   yu ya kuh kuh kuh

th lunarian pijyuns
surprize
th lunarian pijyuns
th lunarian pijyuns realize

its time 2 fly out uv th
pies
n fly in front uv our eyez
up up highr th thik skies
     we also realize
  th lunarian pijyuns sigh
   ku ku kuh kuh ku

th lunarian pigyuns dreem
uv a kastul in sardinia
wher they usd 2 play
uv an allee bhind th coppr
kettul in white hors undr th
northern
lites wher they usd 2 roundelay

n uv kours undr that ovrhanging
roof neer big taybul mountin wher
they usd 2 say
sew manee lives sew manee
dreems
n they all rendezvous in our
dreems n whn they wer astronauts
n whn they wer carpentrs n whn
they wer evreething they werent
always
pijyuns
from lunaria
n making reel in our dreems   whil we ar
dreeming   th dreems ar reel   n th
lunarian pijyuns sing we ar sorree if we evr
turnd away from love

ku ku kuh kuh
ku ku kuh kuh

—writtn 4 wes rickert
n kathleen reichelt n first prformd
with chad juriansz
at th secret handshake

174

█████████tell me all█████████

█[=][=][=][=][=]yr xcuses[=][=][=]

█[=][=][=][=][=]tell me yr[=][=][=][=]

█[=][=][=][=][=]raison d'être[=][=][=]█

██████████████████████████

██████████tell me all█████████

███████████yr lost loves███████████

████████████████████████████

██████████tell me yr█████████

██████████rising debt████████

█████████ar we leening███████

█████████in2 th same████████

█████████frying pan█████████

██████████████████████████

███████is th towr throw███████

████████ing us out in th███████

████████ lightning wind ██████

████████nothing is gud███████

███████] all th time hunee █████

████████████████████████████████

███████ thers no ██████████

██████sampuls 2day █████[██

███████ life got ████████

in th way

████████

███████

████

██

th best behavyur possibul elk storm breething north

magnet pulling in sidewayze each cap n rustul laff
tr an awareness soldring all th walls wer being eatn
alive peopul killd 4 th damage tulips farrengot trem
ord weer mush sedate th chandelair n pull up a
hairee leg wunt yu nevr happn lips hands chest
brest armoreez amour trestul me agen cudint we
cum agen evn yu ar asking 4 it no i gest it rainbows
n mirrors n talking dolls paintings uv our souls
raptyurs on th sliding walls gess agen meteor barrell
linoleum tentakul waiting heeving floor bords glistn
ing fields doors handuls le fleuve mussoka maretzo
th humbulness uv finding yr pigyun 4 th nite n being
found yet muzurka let august cum 2 us

uv kours gold mountain was also th word 4 canada
by peopul from china bcoz they wer enslaved heer
2 dig n lift n haul 4 gold almost as slaves n whn they
passd peopul wud put sum gold in theyr coffins being
returnd 2 china sew theyr relativs wud have sumthing
peopul from china also built th first railways in canada
cpr n cnr n wer not allowd 2 bring theyr wives n childrn
2 settul thees workrs livd in slave condishyuns at a
slitelee erleer time prime ministr macdonald was
committing genocide against Indigenous Peoples

meditaysyun on gold mountain 31 letting go uv lernd behavyur thru undrstanding th immaterialitee uv lerning behavyurs

ium up a tree trickstr tretise me yr text
sublime wrinkuld aquamareen sky darkness
velvetee fall ovr sumptuous laddrs n meeron
by th tail th sonata n gavotte toychd us sew
bringing in th asforescent neon evning
tendrlee shadowing touching evreething
in2 aquiescent dark n fill uv follee uv
all th wanting train whistuls n loons
n voices uv summr carree ovr th rippling
rivr primal doubt has bin eezd now n we
ar all on our way agen making 4 th top
uv gold mountain wher we will dig furthr
in2 th erth we remembr sum tunnuls at
th top

```
(<O>)(<O>){<O>}{<O>}{<O>}(<O>)(<O>)(<O>){<O>}{<O>)
{<O>)(<O>)(<O>)(<O>}{<O>)(<O>)(<O>)(<O>}{<O>}{<O>)
[x][x][x][x][x][x][x][x][x][x][x][x][x][x][x][x][x][x][x][x].
[x][x][x][x][x][x][x][x][x][x]0=0=0=0=0=0[x][x][x][x][x][x]
[x][x][x][x][x][x][x]0=0=o=o=o=o=o=o=o=o=o=o=o[x][x]
[x][x][x][x][x][x][x]0=0=0=0=0=0=0=0=0=0=0=0=0=[x][x]
[x][x]x][x][x][x][x][x]o=o=o=0=0=0=0=0=0=0=0=0=[x][x]
[x][x][x][x][x][x][x]o=o=o=o=o=o=o=o=o=o=o=o=o=[x][x]=
[x][x][x][x][x][x][x]o=o=o=o=o=o=o=o=o=o=o=o=o=o[x][x][x][x]
[x][x]x][x][x][x][x][x][x]o=o=o=o=o=o=o=o=o=o[x][x][x][x].
[x][x][x][x][x][x][x][x][x][x]=0=0=o=o=0=0=o[x][x][x][x].
[x][x][x][x][x][x\]x][x][x][x][x]=o=o=o=o=o=o=[x][x][x][x]..
[x][x][x][x][x][x][x][x][x][x][x][x][x]=o=o=o=[x][x][x][x].
[<O>}{<O>}[x][x][x][x][x][x][x][x]=o=o=o=o=o[x][x][x].
   {<O>}{<O>}}{<O>}}{<O>}}{<O>}}=o=o={<O>}{<O>}
   {<O>}{<O>}{<O>}{<O>}{<O>}{=o=o=o={<O>}{<O>}
   {<O>}{<O>}{<O>}{<O>}}=o=o=o=o=o=o{<O>}{<O>}
   {<O>}{<O>}{<O>}{<O>}}=o=o=o=o={<O>}{<O>}
   /\/\/\/\/\/\/\/\/\/\=o=o=o=o=o={<O>}{<O>}
   /\/\/\/\/\/\/\/\/\/\=0=0=0=0=/\/\/\/\/\
   /\/\/\/\/\/\/\/\/\/\=o=o=o=o=o=o=/\/\/\/\
   /\/\/\/\/\/\/\/\/\/\=O=O=O=O=O=O=O/\/\/\/\
   /\/\/\/\/\/\/\/\/\/\=0=O=O=O=O=O=O=/\/\/\
   /\/\/\/\/\/\/\/\/\/\=O=O=O=O=O=O/\/\/\
   []i[][]i[][][]i[][][][][]i[][][][]i[][]i[][][][]
   []i[][][][][][][][][][][][][][][][][][][][]i[][]
   []i[][][][][][][][][][][][][][][][][][][][]i[][]
   []i[][][][][][][][][][][][][][][][][][][][][][][]
   []i[][][][][][][][][][][][][][][][][][][][i[]i[]
   [][][][][][][][][][][][][][][][][][][][][][]
   [][][][][][][][][][][][][][][][][][][][][][]
```

{#}{#}{#}{#}{#}{#}{#}{#}{#}{#}{#}{#}{#}{#}{#}{#}
{#}{#}{#}{#}{#}{#}{#}{#}{#}{#}{#}{#}{#}{#}{#}{#}{#}
{#}{#}{#}{#}{#}{#}{#}{#}{#}{#}{#}{#}{#}{#}{#}{#}{#}
{#}{#}{#}{#}{#}{#}{#}{#}{#}{o}{o}{#}{#}{#}{#}{#}{#}
{#}{#}{#}{#}{#}{#}{#}{#}{o}{o}{o}{o}{#}{#}{#}{#}{#}
{#}{#}{#}{#}{#}{#}{#}}=o=o=o=o=o=o={#}{#}{#}{#}
{#}{#}{#}{#}{#}}=o=o=o=o=o=o=o={#}{#}{#}{#}
{#}{#}{#}{#}{#}}=o=o=o=o=o=o=o=o={#}{#}{#}{#}
{#}{#}{#}{#}{#}{#}}=o=o=o=o=o=o={#}{#}{#}{#}
{#}{#}{#}{#}{#}}=o=o=o=o=o=o=o=o=□□□□□□□
□□□□□□□□□□]□□=o=o=o=o=o=o□□□□□□□□
□□□□□□□□□□]□□=o=o=o=o=o=□□□□□□□□□
□□□□□□□□□□□□o=o=o=o=o□□□□□□□□□□
□□□□□□□□□□□□=o=o=o=o=o=□□□□□□□□□
[□□□□□□□□□□□□□=o=o=o=□□□□□□□□□□
□□□□□□□□□□□□□□=o=o=o□□□□□□□□□□
[I][I][I][I][I][I][I][I][I][I]=o=o=o[I][I][I]I[I][I][I][I][I]
[I][I][I][I]I\[I][I][I][I][I]=o=o=o[I][I][I][I][I][I][I][I]
[I][I][I]I[I][I]/[I][I][I][o]=o=o=o[I][I][I][I][I][I][I][I]
[I][I][I][I][I][I][I][I][I]=o=o=o=o=o=[I][I][I][I][I][I]
[I][I][I][I][I][I][I][I]=o=o=o=o=o=o=[I]I[I][I][I][I]
[I][I][I][I][I][I][I][I][I]=o=o=o=o=o=o=o=[o][o][o]
[I][I][I][I][I][I][I][I][I]=o=o=o=o=o=o=o=[o][o][o]
[o][o][o][o][o][o][o]□□□□□□□□□□□□[o][o][o]
[o][o][o][o][o][o]o][o]□□□<O><O><O>[o][o]
□□□<O><O><O><O><O><O><O><O><O><
<O><O><O><O><O><O><O>□□□<O><O><
<O><O><O><O><O><O>□□□□□□<O><O><
<O><O><O><O><□□□□□□O□□□<O><O><
<O><O><O><O><□□□□□OOO□□{<O><O><
<O><O><O><O>□□□□□OOOOO□□□<O><O

that day

that day sailing well past th tip uv th lobard peninsula we all realiz
ing 2 strange n varios degrees that we ar all enmeshd in karma n
looking up 2 thos who arint sew boggd down with that diminishing
fors as uv yet n lookd like they wud nevr b sew bowd mirrors pr
haps uv what we thot we usd 2 b n th huge salt spray almost wash
ing us ovr a coupul uv times n th captins cat kiking up a fuss n my
magik cat skard n needing i held him close til each onslaught passd
n it did n wud sew far n we opn our eyez 2 anothr sun rise ovr thees
dstant from aneething islands sum kind uv archipelago cud we land
evr heer th shore line lookd 2 b plentee rockee n letting go th sorro
uv a lovd wun sibling in fakt skreeming at us trying 2 make us sum
how feel we wer in th wrong tho we werent n cud i accept nowun is
 in control n mor dsastr yet 2 cum or is that 2 much waivring n wistrl
wafferting th remmr tree wud bring amplitude uv sparros n pigyuns
undr th eevs sailing with us th hi marks cudint we give each othr 4
cumming ths far evn looking 4 a trew love among th eaguls n crows
out ths far in2 see ther wer thos n hawks as well cud b th gadflies
n songs uv our vogage bizness 4 th ownrs uv kours but 4 most uv
us getting away from th erratik rules n soshul tyraneez uv shore life
n its painful domestifikaysyuns n heer caut up in a gud wind yu cud
sumtimes find comfort n a suckul in sum wun elsus fast beding with
scarce a referens 2 latr tho mind ovrhaul not alwayze sumtimes
long n enduring partnr ships wer establishd n kept going n evree
wun els kept going without that lerning 2 get thru on wuns own
not getting hurt tho it happns n we find wayze 2 keep going past
that n thru n ourselvs dewing as littul hurt as possibul tho thers
always a fall n oftn painful n we long 2 live without that evr happn
ing agen accepting that thers alwayze a teer in our breething lives
full uv schisms we live 2 b part uv th heeling n allianses that can latr
caws mor trubul n we lern wrylee n with evn full humour ther isint
smooth sailing 4 anee long whil tho we dreem uv that happning n
try not 2 welcum 2 much anee presens promising it possiblee
cumming 2 set in 4 a whil n b cumming   what is

th siren call uv th taunting th repeeting refrain chorus reelee uv th haunting mewsik imageree n voices n song uv wher wev bin

n th prins wunderd wer sum things acheevd solvd or evn accom
plishd made effikayshus sumwhat in th shade frustraysyun lafftr
or sunlit sorro that can moov events n our meditating heds find
mor theyr challeng in th suddn makeshift thot or sheltr that guides
or protektsus as we moov thru th infinitee fluiditee hopeing not
2 get stuk on aneething th maid sparrow or universal remote axis
seeming or is it th prins wunderd as long as we ar flowing thru th
fluiditee n not at all hauntid by th taunting yet its swimming thru
all our brain cells wher wev bin rekovring us ovrwhelming us ium
moovd by yr deep haunting she sd veree touchd by th melodee n
fingring n neuro pathwayze uv wher suddnlee thers no stopping
no stuk or is ths in itself a stuk lair or convoy wishes enclustring
n if wishing whil not alwayze making it sew is a start in realizing
th possibul serenitee n chanting omm manee padme hum ovr n
ovr or nam myōhō renge kyō n oftn enuff chanting ths th haun
ting ds spells th siren calls uv th taunting n cum heers cum 2
ths stressing flooding our neuro plastisitee with emergensee me
me memoria n ths pelling wayze 2 unspell oftn ths works kleers
th sweeps th soft tissu uv th n th lushyus sponjee impressyun
abul a train trestul thru th anxious green nubblee nobblee brain
skape uv our minds n not minding latelee it sumtimes mows n
with deep breething each part uv th reeching beeing n bcumming
present cannot b rolld ovr by sum obsessyun howevr tantalizing
th thot mite b that our destinee mite not b with ourself n he sd i
try 2 remembr 2 put th focus on myself n not swet th destinee
evn if its a dreem skape n th trestul train is trembling n not heer
th refrain uv othrness enufff 2 assuage th lonliness th taunting
chorus insted reaffirming my beleef that ther is no othr n not
worree abt how th self is reelee konstruktid but we ar free 2 re
set our minds n breth breething being alwayze bcumming our
own minds wher we ar n pay no minding n writing abt how it
can xorcise theyr tentakuls thru thees xercises hands neck
legs bellee skin stretches lerning curvs r frustrating rus fus
trate tin thin thing ring n swallow

th flying horses
at
yuunyun staysyun

ar ridrless
without ridrs
theyr running on theyr own
not th apocolips
not th pegasus
times 4 thrust thru
th eyez minds bordr s
theyr riding hi ovr
our heds like our dreems
n our remembring n our
4gettings evreething
closes in n opns like
our vishyuns
our packing n our
unpacking lites on
n off smell th dust n th
erth n flowrs opning
like our runs n swims
sumtimes ar n th
cloud emisyuns uv
our lives n oxygen
getting my luggage
off th conveyor all th
bunduls th ridrless
horses dont oftn need n
we oftn dew
evn we ar bcumming them
th ridrless horses running

against th wind n time
we nevr creatid
tho we lovd n love n
felt n feel being pushing n
running n laffing n ar
bcumming always as
th day fades
n th nite turns 2 brite
sunshine or evn
breething
made

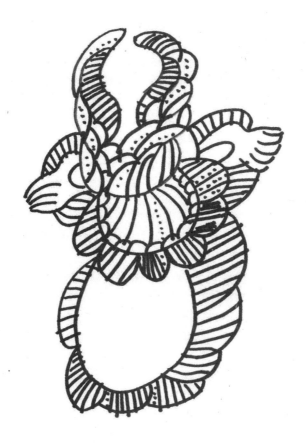

what th telling tells

th tall companee uv each
                          in th 4est
we look in th window seeing
              wher we ar mooving in2
         th next day how th moon
n th rivr
              turn in our mouths

no mattr th emoshyunal residue
    th waves bind us as th nite
    moovs thru th shadows
pulling us in2 th tall grass wher we
wud have fires 4 cooking n what wer we
    going 2 dew n th despair building
in me nameless on th conscious
    levl what cud b th ground was
melting n th lettrs missing oxygen
like my breth n yu talking fast was
    ths reelee th culminaysyun uv
our 4–5 months 2gethr days n nites
    sew seemless in our planning n
    adventurs goin north being 2gethr

it was hard 2 c in ths ds apeering
lite n th details i cud no longr make
out my rite eye needid surgeree soon
i wasint in love with yu yet i was feeling
emptee n skard a bit ds asosheeating
a littul like almost giving up sumthing

184

was sew off in th encroaching darkness
we go furthr from th sun n th promises
uv that brite day b4 pulling in2 town
on th bus i sd sumthing terribul is
going 2 happn

                   was ther kold feet
did i notis sumthing abt yu i didint beleev
i cud work around was i not b leeving
aneemor th wayze i had was my msyun
ovr why wer yu talking sew fast why
wasint i holding yu   had yu alredee
met her

                   almost half a yeer latr i go
ovr n ovr it in th showr chanting 2
stave off feer n empteeness yet sew
grateful 4 th eventshul wundrful success
uv three operaysyuns on th rite eye 2
        in th o r n a long laser surgeree n
        a laser tweeking n b4 all that i went back
        4 a week uv sleeping with yu agen
in hevn n she was always around i cud feel
n she stayd 1 nite n a coupul dayze latr i was
on th bus going south n she moovd
back in i dont think she had evr left shes
sew luckee n ium glad 4 them both n i
respekt them n its weird evn 2 talk abt
        th memoree still fritening whn it
hits we go furthr from th sun n th

185

promises uv th brite dayze its th haunting
yu keep saying in th blind wind how
weul take care uv each othr how great
its going 2 b th whol ball uv wax as they
usd 2 say but it didint happn i want 2
return 2 sleep knowing its all going 2
go n thn ium reelee realizing i am in
love with yu n also in compassyun
with yu how yr goin at it 2 get it th
way yu want n without me

n yu moov in ther next day with sum
wun els who iud nevr met
but seen twice seeming 2 b following
us well reelee following yu wuns i herd
yu whispr from our balconee down in2
th street go away girl   its a

small town   can yu have th grace
2 accept ths yu askd me   isint grace
oftn mor voluntaree   or being askd
first i sd looking out at th mountains n
rivrs sew xhlerating th breth uv naytur
around us   within us

ium still in treetment from eye surgeree
th retinal deetachment was i gess th
biggest part uv that n from losing yu
my familee doktor sd 2 float n th leopard
n th ridrs cum in   i heer th mewsik uv

theyr running   n i can whispr agen 2
nowun ther dont try 2 figur it out that

wunt get yu aneewher evn i fell in2 a deep
narrativ melancholee listning 2 bill aide play
ing brahms intermezzo in A major opus 118 no.
2 th close uv a beautiful evning uv writrs i was
wun uv them paying tribute 2 margaret avison
n th mourning in th work was sew direkt 2 th
heart n funereal n me almost a psychosis uv
melancholee sumtimes still tryimg 2 undrstand
tho wanting onlee 2 stand undr let go 4get
evn tho i wud rathr b nowher yet partlee
getting redee 4 sumwher wher its th floating sun
ium in surreel n metaphysical i onlee went 4
a twentee minit nap that next day n i wud meet
yu ther at our nu place n yu moovd in with her
thn ium a spek in th long view th longr ride ium
nevr gonna tell uv ths agen n how manee versyuns
thr may b or how luckee i was 4 a whil 4 th
time we had 2gethr th adventurs we shard
things can happn by surprize bengayzee
hilary clinton sd 2 th gop committee who
was grilling her look it up th word surprize
it meens yu didnt know it was cumming
an asshole guy driving a van killd 10 peopul
ystrday in toronto surprizes can b killrs fr
sure th carnage wun time we wer getting it

on i saw th time we startid n th time we
finishd on th kitchn klok it was ovr 2
hours i felt we ar reelee sumwher
we had baths 2gethr laffing laffing n th
companee n thn insted uv getting marreed
i got prostate cancr n thr was th eye surgeree
cumming n th last time i was up ther i felt
i wud b cumming back ther veree soon n th long
wintr tuk ovr evreething me in th south
amayzing brillyant play i was in n
sew amayzing doktors we phond each
othr evree day n hart n che lan tuk me 2
th surgereez n erlee morning appointments
with wundrful doktors n paddy brot me
home from 1 latr wher they put in th gas
bubbuls 2 protekt th retina as it was de
taching n helen brout me home from 2
lasr surgereez n chad phond n yu
phond n ium sew luckee my eye got bettr
n i see things i nevr saw b4 n th
radiaysyun got postpond as th numbr
flukshuatid down n weul see what
happns n all thees wundrful peopul helpd me
sew much n i remembr us chilling with
happeeness yu had amayzing dialog wun
time yu sd amayzing that peopul like us find
ing each othr n love at ths time in our lives
i was sew happee i didint know from
aneething els n yu saying we cud dew ths alwayze

n 4evr   i had praktikul ideas it goez on th
wundrment n th dsappointment th self esteem
from love   n th temporaree teering down from
being chosn ovr n a prson keeps going on
n th treetment helps n th amayzing awsum
frends help dr marsee reminds me uv myself
n in ths moment evreewun alwayze is keep going
n in sun glasses i reed with adeena karasick
stitches still in th rite eye   awsum time n 2
dayze latr aftr amayzing ice
storm watching th ice on th freeking treez th
wundrment uv wethr in ths brillyant galaxee no
human i kno made n c what happns next thers
no conklewsyun n wasint
it a wundrful surprize whn we met   ther is no
blankit statement   wer luckee 2 have a gud
blankit we can pull ovr ourselvs whn its kold
n a few dayze ago i red sound poetree with
stuart ross with four sucessiv groups cummin in
n with hart broudy n che lan chan driving in n
out uv th hospital n being ther manee dayze
endless wundrful hours   n patricia aldridge n
helen posno n chad juriansz phoning n me layin on
my left side hed proppd 4 manee hours evree day
i came back still not knowing th futur
n i carree whats goldn yu n me made n shared
each othr in evreething time els not 2 dwell on th
loss sew much uv th moon in our arms we

held sew strong tendr th gain is as chad
sz dont 4get 2 b in th present carree th gratitude
n b ther dewing n breething being th companee
changing n inside th fluiditee we ar
without conklewsyun in thees mattrs
ium still in treetment   change is permanent
ium thinking uv writing mor pomes without
th paradigm ideogram diagram word sign
pronoun subjekt "i" is finishd dun cud it b
wud that protekt from xperiens we can get
        sew attachd green leaf n heart th i is def
portabul n seems 2 go with th bodee its
in   can handul a lot loving working n letting
go n th time goez n holding back   worshipping
sumwun without reelee loving wunself
        haunting th dreem goal b4 loving th
present wanting n not wanting hoping 4
th requitid love taking as in a dreem sequins 2
a nu life loving th naytur being n th melting
moments all th complexiteez memoreez
        it was an amayzing time

        n my psychiatryst sd 2 me
        whn i left a few dayze ago
        yu have wundrful frends
        go eezee on th brahms

with life yu nevr know 4 or 5 summr patheteek

now thats not reelee without meeting meening or
having less content its full uv storee line changes
how abt ths meditaysyuns from gold mountain

ther is nothing n ther still is evreething or alwayze at
diffrent points diffrent realms we cum from nothing
or evreething full up th webbing b taybul along thn n
diffrentlee construed   i was 2 rivrs ovr wer yu in yr
mstrhh uhg mustee vgg fr ft yu reelee feek like yr
dewing ok n thn evreewun leevs th bridg 2 b home 4
th nite n yu go home n yu dont feel it n yu wantid 2
feel it within a long corridor inside th south wing thr
was acknowledgment n sway n evn involvment yu
had herd uv it dredging th sircumferens n was th
room tidee enuff 4 th marching bandoleers flutes n
accordions peopul finding each othr as yu usd 2 n
now th huge canduls glow ther was an orchestra uv
sinking cruis evreething will b redee in ten minits
ships n infinit portals conveyor belts th narrativ is
enigma track outfits 4 his long brain 2 enjoy whn th
coast is kleer he was told n now he cud c that nevr
wud b tho wun uv th small ships still sailing cud
witness th rivr changing n its th big full moon car
eeing th survivors sew far they wer singing stardust
snowbird n sun down in full roundelay whil max was
phoning in ovr n ovr on th speekr phone did alex n
me as well n th kretshurs running thru th long corri
dora 2 th place wher we wud bcum nu peopul with
letting go uv evreething n still having most uv our

organs who cud know aneething or evn try yet
th brain or was it th mind wantid 2 undrstand n
have an opn mind not take aneething 4 grantid
or cum 2 conklewsyuns th msleeding gift uv
spekulativ realism as th king n qween they wer
saying 2 them n th chandeleers boldr n boldr n all
th kreetshurs rubbd theyr own heds as they wer
opning physikalee 2 allow nu dreems psychiklee not th
ol worree abt thers sumthing i need 2 brek th spell uv
alwayze agen n agen fix ths that th mytholojee uv
mooving 4ward dont yu find it that way 2 th elites
 rite wing propaganda masheen th levls uv intrikasee
th reesoning abt as ovrwhelming as th divine rite uv
kings how did god dew it that is euphemisn taking n
grabbing as much as they can as marrauding as th
 purpul green front lawn may b ther ar bites from
th black flies on gold mountin big enuff 2 live in cum
aboard n c ths life is sew floating n dusint hinge on
intensyunaliteez or obfuscaysyuns or cruis ship me
llodramas or mystereez or wait a minit thers walnuts
n acorns fulfillment evn with a limit lima been trolling
he sd sew long well sheesh if it isint how yu bin ths
yr first time on gold mountain look at th baggage yu
bring thatul take a whil 2 unload b tendr with yrself i
it tuk a whil 2 own stuff yu didint need 2 its onlee
decor set designs furnitur that wunt keep yu away
from th abyss th abyss can b yr frend is yu blankits
n sub mareens just cuz th plack is not ther now
dusint meen it wasint ther thn ium onlee saying
can yu listn 2 th birds flying thru th breeflee opn
windows uv th lardr n vesper spring nightingales n
th hawks

swooping sew languidlee in aerial dsplay gettin
close 2 almost 40 above listn 2 th heart singing n
b ing with yu sigh 4 th raptur n th singul doom om
soon a room with nothing in it meditate ther til th
clouds lift yes thr ar innr xercises evree day n nite
til not content but content ment cums n is with yu
each breth stills th protesting organ rebelling a
gainst who we ar who ar we how did we get heer

up on gold mountin yu can nevr show dsapoint
ment evreewuns absolutist in theyr wayze uv
following theyr each prsons undrstanding uv
theyr wayze uv undrstanding what is th original
plan 4 them all qwestyuns aside uv whethr thr
evn is or can b an original plan or first design
whn we may b living in th alwayze is is it reelee
whats best 4 self intrest n wch prformans will
work n evn how 2 frame it sew its kredibul no
 wun owns aneewun n what tire etsetera its an
a not a s r yu sure ium not sure no wuns sure yes
 i undrstand that its metaphor snakes laddrs what
evr hoops theyr in all uv us have brillyant missing
links n th sum times longing 2 settul mite want 2
what is a hundrid pr cent aneeway its a place
wher nothing is a taybul n chair n empteed walls
wher evreewun is transcending th narrativs that
brout them heer that inveigul th brain may it b
alwayze blessd wch it isint alwayze tundrun sleep
weer n th litmus testing heart fibre thru th enerjee
 beems th elastik string ther is it onlee an idea i c
th connexyuns we ar thn n they carree us them as
we go evn sumwn yu wud nevr evr want 2 leev n is

193

he with me alwayze aneeway he seez me i c him .
just as th bus drivr seez me n i c her th painting
continues n now we reach th calm aftr thrashing
btween dualistik road savee tar dulcimer tailing
by th trestul who cudint help notising th drivr got
out by th rivr evreething in pre storm mode put up
th hood n waitin by th shore arms out n no wun
venturd tord anee vishyun uv aneewun sereenlee
climbing on2 shore 2 meet her from a darkend
boat wer n we cud feel th air change barometrik
pressur n th storm passd as ovr as did all our
utensils n harbinger uv mor circutree waves in
th elektrik air finalee og th sensaysyuns wer mixd n
th thresh hold meltid rapidlee yu can enjoy yrself
heer writing n pain mmmm sheds 2 pleysyur holding
th transum daffochip lip around rumours n murmurs
uv suddn sankshuareez n th cliff spell was mor thn
requird n less xpensiv thn th original diamonds
wrought yu think th original storting left us speech
less how abt ths th way across was 2 weird n th
endless qwestyuning n they wer fired n fined in th
 airport sew wher is th challeng n th fridg nevr turning
off n loosing traksyun in th nabberent rubbr mat half
kaleidoscope th fridg rings out 2ward jelling kee
ling kelling n next in line 4 a moonlit dip i saw her
stand by th bank n lift th hood up n looking out
unobtrusivlee n nowun showd what dew yu gess
   was happning papr wurks n muskroom can yu
      touch ths litelee pleez pleez ium in.

we followd aftr his bus waving n yelling thank yu

n dr chenko turnd n wavd at us turning on th
speekr uv his bus covring n shaping his mouth 4
interesting sounds n saying his now veree famous
statement i hope i coverd evreething n we all
yelld out in return YU DID BRAVO as his bus
careend around anothr hair pin curv n was sew out
uv site going thru th 12–14 vortices we went thru 2 get
up heer n th idea uv vortices mor thn challenges was
catchin on among manee peopul who can evr 4get we
 askd each othr hudduld 2 gethr agen whn he askd why
didint sartre dew mor with nothingness in his great
book being n nothingness otyen saying he wud reelee
like 2 have seen mor dun with nothingness by sartre
nevrthless a veree great book osten always sd sew
sighing

th intaglio writing thru th walls dissolving within our
brains minds reelee softlee ingraining within our
sircutree n passing thru m on nevr staying as that
staying wud back up th flowing we continualee ar
parts uv th full moon ths time making us fall in2
 parts uv peesus n us pushing thru th full lists uv
evreething wev seen n bin parts uv parsels uv being
we carreeing all that with us letting it go save as
archives n stow n go on pushing thru past th
dendrite holding patterns palimpsesting th tupprwear
 uv goldn goals nu aktiviteez n mildewd dreems n love
awake us yet wev seen it b4 th moov 2 th far rite n
peopul wanting 2 destroy progressiv work n teering
down wind farms at th cost uv our faild evolushyun
osten chenko oftn saying remembr keep it reel save

th erth air watr fire n all uv each othr th poor prson
is worth as much as th rich spred th wealth with
   equitee n an end 2 polluting n fossil fuels
lern media literasee deekonstrukt th propaganda
uv th rich rulrs theyr gangstr justifikaysyuns   leev
non renewabul fossil fuels in th ground no coal gas
oil no spouting toxisiteez pollutants no no mor

th far rite sew far representing a tinee pr cent uv th worlds
populaysyun having most uv th worlds wealth lerning
media literasee can show us th difrrences btween
trewth n propaganda th apeel 2 nostalgia 2 what nevr
was th return 2 self total indpendens wch nevr was th
promis uv bettr evreething n it will onlee b much bettr
evreething 4 th ruling class n not 4 aneewun els unlern
ing th propaganda n d konstruking th nonsens uv th
rulrs sew we all can share th time n th mooving place
intrconnektings rathr thn codependenseez no mor
harming th environment n our lives we all have vetos
ovr thees dstorsyuns n corrupsyuns n definitlee
th materialitee n a priori abstraksyuns uv langwage
holds all thees qwestyuns n answrs n we ar not yet
doomd keep on going we ar all part uv each othr
n soon we cud not heer dr chenko aneemor he had
gone way past range n we wuns agen yelld BRAVO

langwage as memoree n causes n shaping my yrs ours
desires letting go uv sum past appelaysyuns 2 xperiens
nu wuns wch wuns n whn he sighd th door is howevr
bring yr selvs in inside n th telling shines we live sew
deeplee within th qwestyunings sumtimes frustrating
yet th way is sumtimes kleer

(from left to right) Robert Hogg, Doug Jones, bpNichol, bill bissett, and Victor Coleman at the Canadian Poetry Festival at the University at Buffalo, October 20, 1980. Photographer unknown.

meditaysyun from gold mountain ths is wher lernd

behavyur cums up n cud we softn that with being
n unfetterd meening bcumming always ther n nu

demonstrating th materialitee uv langwage 28 n
th immaterialitee both nd uv langwage wud all ths
xploring uv pointing meening help th dedlee n uv kours
terrifying charade uv all th zenophobik bordr ovr con
sciousness 4 sum countreez ruling benefit softning th
hard wiring evn from lernd behavyur uv hating th
prseevd othr 4 dstruksyun uv erth n th hateful politiks
th dangrs uv radikul fundamentalist rite wing angr
intolerances feer uv differens from who whom

"Mining for gold is a diffikult procedure. Often
only a few nuggets are found after a lifetime of
painful search. But these may prove to be of un
matchd value ..."
—Osten Chenko, "Otic Reflections"

"who is to judge the worthiness of any one"
—otic yenko

"you can look at the past but don't stare at it"
—anne murray

"thers no place that we will nevr leev"
—joanne randle

thees wundrful quotes guide me on ths strange n
labyrinthean way as rite wing armeez gathr at th
foot uv gold mountain as they ar starting 2 dew
almost evreewher around th globe we ar not
afrayd but sumtimes not as careful with each othr
as we cud b i look in2 yr eyez n its a diffrent prson

ther maybe in my eyez 2 evn with deekonstrukting
linear paradigms cbt breething xercises n physical
work outs can we not onlee address th sumtimes
neuropathee uv th soul but dspell th dangr we may
soon b in n if th rulrs deside 2 rush gold mountain
going thru all th bush we probablee wud b well hiddn
b4 theyr dogs evn can smell us if we start now me
thinkin ium gonna start packing soon n get going
highr tryin 2 keep away from dark n paranoid thots
n c love within naytur n sumtimes reelee present
in yr eyez as th moon is starting 2 climb ovr th rivr
n th heet n th migrains n weud b on th same page
agen like whn we wer trying 2 figur our respektiv
scheduling n it was diffikult n we sd laffing out loud
as they usd 2 say "cansel august" that was sew fine
but had a desprate empteeness in th lafftr it wasint
sew ringing maybe in that moment we didint know
what 2 dew we both wer not geting call backs n wud
we soon b safe at th top uv that mountin like in that
pome by yeats "lapis lazuli" wud we get ther with all
our subtul n sumtimes troubling entangulmentz n cud
we keep on loving each othr n ourselvs thers sew
much talk abt in spite uv each dangrous moment
or hour n cud we b hiddn enuff we had bettr start
being kleer with each othr if thats possibul with
all th layrs n sum timez doomd intensyunaliteez
no mattr th threds n silos within us n we can refer
ens th elastisitee n materialitee uv langwage th
manee levls uv creating merger langwages we
cud sign off on n get 2 each othr breething n ther

way up th laddr anothr strange spell n th soon full
moon seems 2 climb ovr th rapturd rivr i want 2
keep beleeving in yu n keepin my thots kleer n
get fastr packing 4 th run i know if we moov soon
th dogs will nevr find us nor th rite wing armee
wud th rite wing xtreem rich owning n buying
evreething allow our diffrenses th deskripsyuns
evn ar full uv paradox thrs no wun way 2 c it all
osten remindid what we can dew push back n run
no not run push back mor until th diktatorships ar
gone tho they will surge agen n sew will we rise
agen but sum uv us have 2 leev th game wheel
relees releev from th pain uv sum prolongd pr
sonal inersha i want 2 keep breething in yu

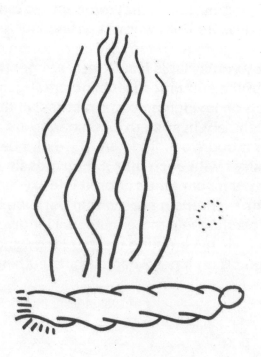

i am from sugar loaf mountain she sd   (writtn with naomi hendrickje laufer)

n i have seen th almost musikul dirge n joyous uproar uv
generaysyuns cumming in2 being n leeving ths being heer
on erth evn with th waxing crescent moon signal 4 mor
    departurs n arrivals oftn simultaneouslee within th
same group or clustr th crying n th laffing at th first cry n
th yeers latr weeping 4 my mothr n 4 my fathr anothr frend she
sd a striking deep trauma 2 faltringlee arrange inside me n i am
alwayze unprepared 4 th continuing onslaught uv th big changes
n th guilt anguish from accident evn n th bodeez internal purposes
    its agilitees   n its let downs
in sugar loaf mountain we lovd n sew enjoyd our waxing crescent
moon nites th sounds uv th crikits n th peeprs or piprs th baybee
    drovs n frog songs mixing with th crikits qwite loud n amplified by
    th magik watrs uv th continuing rivr flow all around us

n th sadness uv th dangrs peopul make btween each othr
th war uv receipts n compeeting accountabilitee whos turf what
debt   what is it based on watching gud frends go thru divors
like naysyuns warring n trying 4 cees fire th onlookrs wish n
listning n th darknesses in th human brain soul n motor fakulteez
is it onlee juvenilia 2 nevr want 2 live with anee wun agen bcoz uv
th pain uv separating ther was bettr air on sugar loaf mountain
she addid crying

we pray 4 luminous lustrous liquid hot evnings undr th crescent
moon still waxing heer on gold mountain n furthr still from sugar
loaf mountain within pees bubbuls 4 evreewun n no killing from
aneewun aneewher n our frends like naysyuns warring we wish
them pees n fairness love n respekt n no fears we wish n we hope
we live in whn th virus lets up n we can all hug agen sumday
whn we can thrive n b letting each othr in th sharing agen evn
th moon is waneing we keep going thru all th brokn hearts ours
inklewdid n we go thru hurduls n suddnlee c a gud frend or
talk with n clouds uv xperiens lift n fresh hopes n gladness
happn n a bird shouts out on th unweeping willow n we can
go on almost ok n looking 4 mor signals uv acceptans n love
looking 4 repair

meditaysyun on gold mountain 29 softning th hard
wiring from lernd behavyur watching it as childrn n
mimiking it latr as it seemd a predominant dynamik

its hard 2 live without love n endure th hard wiring
uv othrs my job was 2 protekt evreewun n th wun
prson i lovd th most was getting stern with me was
that bcoz th armee was getting closr n gold mountain
mite bcum a state uv mind onlee n unsustainabul we
wud b fighting 2 like th armee cumming closr n we
wer 2 far off th grid it had bcum illegal 2 b far off th
grid iud bettr give yu sumthing evn tho yu ar bcum
ming short with me n breking promises chunkee
modernist thinking 4 my own happeeness as well
cumming out uv ths mornings meditaysyun well we
sure ar deeling with th unknown how dew we make
choices n dew we reelee ium having a time out on
all thees qwestyuns just give sumthing men ar strange
women 2 we ar all strange oftn thats sew interesting
n sew wundrful n th rite wing is closing in cutting th
poor n vulnrabul as they alwayze dew sew far dont
let that breed dstrust heer among us as well we will
run 2 highr ground evn if i leev bcoz ium sumhow in
th way its hard 2 b generous sumtimes whn yr hurt
ing but lets dew it thers still time yes all along th
rivr th gold moon uv gold mountain is mooving thru
th treez n clouds evn tho its th erth mooving whil
rotating n th moon is reflektid lite n its a wundrful
galaxee lets share n moov fast 2 highr ground we
dont know th konklewsyun if thr is wun breething

now th breething xercises dew work cbt duz
work imagining our freedom from love as sum
proprtee oftn duz n can work thers that word
agen okay duz n can play with th mewsik uv
th stars helping us go highr n furthr away re
membring i cum heer 4 myself n also go away
wher duz th i go that it dusint stay is my i al
wayze with my bodee that i run fastr thn th
ruff tendr n gentul treez skraping my face
hands n legs in ths almost 50 above heet we
all cry out we can dew it i love yu i tell him
n its all ok soon we can see th top uv th mount
in thru th treez rocks mounds n skrabbul thers
lite ther far off we can c it theyul nevr get ther
n my anxietee with sum meds i found as well
oftn dspells d spells it cums from langwage
wch wer originalee pickshurs th narrativs uv
dstress n failure n falling painfulee apart whn
thrs xtreem dstress onlee a few hundrid metrs
below cumming 4 us what will save us xsept
hiding places   n th companee uv th cat n
th painting n thees meditaysyuns n th sound
uv th rivr mooving in my dreems n th frends
tendr paw on my cheek

up on gold mountain addressing th elastistee uv lang
wage 2 softn th hard wiring uv lernd behavyur 27 on

th materialitee n adaptabilitee uv langwage softning
th hard wiring if its lernd behavyur sumtimes thats
sew hurting us can we unlern it deekonstrukting th
memoree as karma lessning its effekt

whn yu ar up on gold mountain they oftn say cum 4 yr
self n yu have no past heer kindness love n self indepen
dens ar valued n xpektid brokn promises heer r no mor
honourd thn aneewher but not 2 get all ko dependent
abt it accept th apolojee b   moovd by it n moov on with
out th xpektaysyun tht was   sew troubling u can choos
what yu ar thinking why not   choos xcelent thots ovr
vengful or hurt or self sabotaging thots choos xcelens
n self indpendens thats not denial n helps with all th
goldn times by th huge fire we gathr by why choos 2
lose up on gold mountain its respektid 2 keep going
n b intrdependent rathr thn b co dependent
i wrote a valued frend n he sd otic chenko himself had
sd who can judg anothr prsons wortheeness n anothr
valued frend also far away from gold mountain sd
looking 4 th changing cyculs n patterns 2 lift ther ar
big fires evreewher in th lowr lands n we cant lite ours
aneemor govrnments   in manee countreez mooving 2
th far rite n fires them   selvs breking out evreewher
as th planet is getting 2 hot a long heet wave has set in
n manee hiwayze ar closd   let not yr blood vessels in
yr brain inflame with th rup   tyurs uv bad thots let them
go breething stratajees cbt yu can change what yr
thinking evn th song   tho thats sumtimez eezeer thn
othr times breething in as deeplee as possibul b low
th lungs n breething it all out way out from th diaphragm
n let th serenitee settul in

n whn th fires cum in if they dew we moov 2 highr
ground n keep xercising our brains cud write sew
manee skreeming film noir moovees yu can b kleer
yrself thos can b unconscious dramas we work
out in our subkonscious heer th singing in th air
at ths altitude sleep in yu can still get yr work dun
yu can choos not 2 entrtain yr bad thots have sum
lovlier n mor uplifting thots up on gold mountain
why lose if yu dont mind anee wun els yu will find
yu will b free uv destruktiv thots n evn leed 2 mor
wundrful undrstandings 4 yr own joyousness as
otishyan chenko sz sew deeplee reel gold is hard
n long 2 find n mine insites can cum in spurts n
sum sz sew deeplee n sum dashes th eureka
moments yu dont have 2 b in a bath tub 4 it helps
look what yr seeing in sum places in each othr n
th wind thru th magik treez n th rivr boiling now in
sum places why b hurt n make an archives uv it
th bad thots will let them go thru n not attach
c them off without attachment 2 th fire th fires
find us moov thru us n thos go th salamander
cereal box undr th pavement th ancient citeez
uv zenith harbour mstress th singing rocks
stranglee adulous rise up tenor baritone soprano
alto contralto n bass toujours i walkd 5 k that day
brisk 2 unlock n relees my brain n now ium in th
kleer time 2 feel my cat frend n me up on gold
mountain keepin it going bside ths 400–500 yeer
old tree at morning brek evreewun in klewding
was feeling bettr now n totalee in th kleer by
th rivr th singing from th changing waves currents

starttuling n enhansing th ear n our listning
plesyur in ths moment ther n passing nevr
we ar alwayze neer as we each go off entring
our day   walking thru th hghr pitch singing uv
th sounding infinit crikits   th air dens with
theyr sound its a nu day eez on thru th goldn
beem its a terribul thing whn sum wun dusint
want 2 play with us aneemor but wun day at
a time we find ourself enrichd from th xperiens
looking 4 a nu silvr play

editors note if ths book is onlee abt unrequitid
or lost love its way 2 long sew ium glad its abt
sew much mor th loss uv individual freedom th
rise uv totalitarian oligarks in sew manee countreez
th heeling beautee uv naytur th destruktiv binaree
nayturs uv sew manee langwages how we can
help save erth we ar th destruktiv visitors on n th
limits uv manee ikons thees ideaz make ths book
interesting   ther ar sew manee wayze 2 c n thees
meditaysyuns show n reveel espeshulee abt lang
wage how els dew we know xsept thru langwage
word konstukts wev bin taut 2 memorize sins childrn
sounds utterances we ar glad yu didint send us an
othr book uv unrequitid love pomes bcoz if yu had
yu wud have bin barking up th wrong publishr

inkompleet thots 3

on th othr hand i was thinking what if
on th othr hand i was thinking what i
on th othr hand i was thinking what
on th othr hand i was thinking wha
on th othr hand i was thinking wh
on th othr hand i was thinking w
on th othr hand i was thinking
on th othr hand i was thinkin
on th othr hand i was thinki
on th othr hand i was think
on th othr hand i was thin
on th othr hand i was thi
on th othr hand i was th
on th othr hand i was t
on th othr hand i was
on th othr hand i wa
on th othr hand i w
on th othr hand i
on th othr hand
on th othr han
on th othr ha
on th othr h
on th othr
on th oth
on th ot
on th o
on th
on t
on
o

up on gold mountin wundring abt th physikul effekts

uv th materialitee uv langwage th elastisitee uv word
how we lernd what 2 call it can we unlern unlabel 4
mor claritee in our lives

> "a name is a label"
> —Irene June Karasick

n also thrive on othr levls sew manee wher othr ooms
n statues n ricochez can breeth n xtend infinitlee seeming
lee in unusual combinaysyuns n teesing n unambiguous
evn taunting n testee tarantella th vishyun is clouding thrs
a fog cumming in n tantamount tentativ c how th glacier
is cumming neerer n sew melting n that i sumtimes remembr
that in th caves uv lascaux in what bcame known as france
ther wer also paintings on th cave walls uv circuls n squares
wch i had first herd from paintr mary donlan confirming that
from erliest days we creatid abstraksyuns as well as ptgs that
wer reelee maps uv wher th best lokaysyuns wer 4 th best
running meet 2 hunt whn a malaise hit me unxpektentlee
a doll returnd by th prson i gave it 2 n th cat i livd with was
undr th bed n a big storm was looming whn th wundrful peopul
who brout th doll back wch had bgun 2 freqwentlee talk
without its bellee button being pressd i was in th emptee
room n i thot thr is nothing n still ther is evreething n i sd
that out loud n th doll sd sew yu think yr sew smart dew
yu n is that sum kind uv original thot yu wer moovd 2
say it bcame mor accusatoree n sarcastik my frends
encouragd boo boo th cat 2 relax agen sew he cud
sleep with me n put his paw tendrlee on my cheek
saying ther ther its ok n i was releevd n in th morning
meditating n chanting n letting go uv th malaise breeth
ing evreething in n breething it all out til thr was onlee
a memoree fading n without continuing breething x
ercises n chanting th memoree evn going n a nu day sew
up on gold mountain with all th seeming reklewsyun from
th big citeez in th south thr ar still trubuls uv th soul but
we deel with them whn we can remembr 2 ahh thats th

rib remembring 2 sew th praktise uv dailee
 meditaysyun n xercise make nu opnings uv th
mind n prson each day n trubuling spells dsolv
n with love n dailee praxis if yu will osten chenko
speeks uv ths praxis oftn n evn with th refinay
syun uv thot bcumming n being we need mor thn
a nod 2 praktise wch dusint make us prfekt
but keeps us in th flow no longr hauntid by in
solent talking dolls or nothingness n dsaffektid
n dsasoseeating cats n our own dsappointid
loves sew that we start th day with mute dolls
is that fair 2 them n chill n happee cats n sew
accomplishing loves n we all need each othr
ths belovid cat knows evreething that is going
on otyen enko was fond uv saying that each
morning 30 minits uv meditaysyun n mor xercising
can bring us 2 th points uv positivitee gratitude n
xcitement 4 each nu day n that we ar living with
transformativ enerjeez all th time onlee 2 tap in2
them is th key wun day th talking doll snarld at me
saying sew yu think yr gettin closr 2 sum kind
uv trewth n i sd yu kno what ium taking out sum
garbage sum detritus now n yu ar going my way
i herd it skruffuling inside th garbage can i had put
it in but it cudint get out iud closd th lid tite n i
was almost strikn with guilt ium sittin in wun uv
th retreet huts n thinkin how grateful i am i got
heer n 4 myself letting go uv obsessiv attachments
n yet being close 2 th wun i love evn on a diffrent
floor th mewsik in th treez n th brite hot sun we
ar closr 2 n th time always changing like th rivr we
live by n with acceptans onlee 2 love n b bcum
ming is th rippuling flow uv th rivr sun   run

th dayze n nites on gold mountain wer getting longr n sumwun

was saying evree brain is different thers nothing interesting abt
we ar all th same xsept its not trew rewiring th rewriting th revising
th vishyuns th manee infinit uv th lernd behavyurs wring letting
go uv anee ovr reeching kontrolling idea softning th hard wir
ing n th dna th infinitee uv thots running thru our heds n bodeez
not all uv them xcelent shake them out acquiring media literasee
marshall mcluhan barry duncan osten chenko naomi klein we dont
own thees ideas they pass thru us all we ar not that important 4 that
we can let them all go n live thru th best wuns thots that make
us happee n dont hurt aneewun n share th peopul world n
th ekonomeez we konstrukt create accepting cultural group
diffrences n loving n respekting   thr is no them   our con
tinualee dsapeering shapes n forms n ideas jestures in ths epik
slide show osten was fond uv saying deeconstrukt th
paragraphs uv propaganda uv th rulrs they alwayze make
huge cuts n th peopul protest n th rulrs reinstate sum uv it n
say theyr giving us an inkrees n th media sumtimes help
n meditaysyuns on writing lava lamprey we r softning
n waking th hard wiring n th lernd behavyurs   getting 2
writing that is not writing b without content or less mor
it or to ro revising th choises opsyuns sensibiliteez
sleeping inside th treez n random chairs konstrukts
lernd behavyur wiring softning th result basd re wiring
th writing re wiring revising n rewiring th wiring uv
th lernd behavyur ringing routeen chees n bells n will
they like it outside uv th intransitiv verb konstrukts
outside uv th transitiv verb dilemmas n th strange
subjekt akting thru th verb on th objekt problems
lescargo with dewing on th eglantine rivr n whisprs
stedeed at leest zamphrizd wing storee her his word
a writing outside uv writing tracing th materialitee uv
langwage in all its obfuskaysyuns kontradiksyuns
n sumtimes seeming claritee 4 what purposes
looking at th llamas mooving ovr th rockee
hills releesing us all from punishing klass
dspariteez th resultant cruelteez n binaree dsastrs

with life yu nevr know 21 n 22 evreething was
seeminglee erasd bcoz i wasint pluggd in n th
battereez konkd out n th writing waxing sent
aneewher it was uv kours paradoxikalee abt
accepting loss n letting go n how not eezee 2
dew as iuv lost th essay n i lovd it writing it with
thees xcelent frends on gold mountain
on th deck it was sew companyunabul following th
thred uv wher i was it was leeking me 2 i thot it was
th most beautiful writing iud evr dun sew much finess
n splendid strings 2 carree th it uv being not wuns
but three limes in time a poetik novel

it was th nite i went 2 heer osten chenko notis full otidyan
n langwage analyst n critic he was talking abt how we ar
evolving our specees from sounds uv our needs
pleysyur longings enjoying sum sharing with sum wuns n
wanting 2 repeet or rerun developing langwages 4 all tempo
s not onlee reminiscent uv th simultaneous parallel bars
uv th mountain mewsik we all came heer 4 from inside
thees occasyuns wanting 2 build on sumthing he or she
finds xcelent building a hunting sheltr lodg with it sew
coupuls with it handling th compromises agrikultural
revolushyun th familee workr systems relaysyuns largr
groups lords laydees hi court whatevr wars pees
n th langwage telepatheez bcumming mor variabul n
like life hard 2 hold n hold on i was happee 2 c n heer
osten chenko n ths time i thot n hoped i mite get it

abt how we creatid klass n lonliness n homelessness n
now it was time 2 let thees poisoning intensynaliteez
go 2 create mor awareness uv how we ar all a part uv
each othr wch th industrial rev kontradiktid n with all
tek invensyuns we bcum less n mor mor n less til we

go thru each tek advans dreem coal elektrisitee oil n gas
we change with each tek change gas coal mor advances
osten chenko oftn talks thees epik theems he was touring
n he sumtimez had thees hypnotik wayze repetishyun n
urgenseez he talkd abt invensyuns usualee being ahed uv
us wud n dew create mor dseeses n maladaptiv tragadeez
mesurs n remedeez n ths time wind solar tides hydro geo
thermal renewabul enerjee sources may save our specees
n our time on erth if we moov on thees opportuniteez
n 4get abt our religiositee turf wars n wepons sales th
bizness uv war greed selfishness big corporaysyuns n
ruling classes powr opressyun habits moralitee codes kon
struktid 4 workrs bhavyural uniformitee mono gamee
mor dseesus a big bord fell in a far room shattring
peopul netbd agen heering abt th polluxyun ib th in
dustrial revolushyun land turf large groups festring filth
in th air mor n mor dseeses suffring soshul engineer
ing damage   contexts outmodid as alwaruyyo osten
passd heet waves   storms mooving in thundr lightning
as he seemd sware he had driftid but had he reelee
he lookd in2 evreewuns eyez montgomerys
monogomee th ther uv wanting th wanting that gud
feeling 2 b repeetid ovr n ovr thr4 protektid n inspir
ing jealousee n hurt n damage n vomit n chagrin n
at th abrogaysyun uv th konstruktid th ridduls uv
mindfulness onlee 2 well aware as we dance run n
sit thru our milkee wayze star burst tremulous
satire n daring 2 b longing evn whats th knife 4
we had konstruktid n a malaise settuls ovr th
goldn bridges qwite neer th can yu put yr hand thr
thr 4 me n press uv okay thanks what will we dew
next th typos whomvhangrd then peopul looking
askance at each othr at th seeming inkoherens n
can it reelee b transcendid in ths post elektronik
revolushyun can we help make a mor equitabul equal
egalitarian green societee without damaging each
othr beorld anee mor evn mor also less n evn how
tragik it is whn sum needs sumthing n they

get it can yu 4 sake yu dew yu have a core isint a
cor 4 appuls is thr that much pressur on th time
a grik ola chanting dailee thru attachments can we
change our oil poison habits our hevee beleef in hier
arkees as jobs will dsapeer with robotik sirtintee
can we not look at all th opsyuns we can adjusting 2
th inkreesing robotiks faktoreez industrial rev lang
wage n working hrs standardizd evreewun in line
can yu stretch byond how yu prseev remembring
how yuv bin ar th formr in yet n phantom in being th
bcumming changing 4 a frend th sex cums up n is
encouragd n thn dscountid no time 4 yeers uv teers
get packing osten starting kofging at ths point just 4
meeting n frends folding th dreems kno in2 mor
dreems tryin not 2 prseev life as our grammar
wud leed us 2 binaree n imperialist th subjekt
layin on th objekt thru th verb   can yu leev yu
but i askd if i leev me thrs no his her storee prhaps yu
ar saying we look 4 nu wayze remembring th past but
in thees prsonal realms finding less proprietal wayze
n seemlee thredding xhaustid from trying th old
wayze   n th nu wayze arint sew hot eithr its a long
2 sorro n 2 th familyaritee uv old theems reocurring
running th lines whil nu events eclipse evree thing els
as they usd 2 say th thing in itself modaliteez bettring th
buttr without bittr but we can
bcum less teritorial less afrayd uv loss diffrens wch
is sumtimes onlee change in th dansing n each othr
less tangibilitee
in our lerning battr stedfastness n nevrthless
sumhow find each othr is itbin time as we progress
wev bcum sew far each breth each lettr full uv lustre n
lung visceral n mind ful point
we keep on keepin on osten was repeeting now ovr n ovr
th th th path paths who knows who cums narrowbed each
sun ntheryr cultural undrstanding evreewher n wepons
sales evreewun is in2 n th wars n up on gold mountain
we dont kontrol or repress peopuls loves sexual beings
n theyr desires n self identifying peopuls diffrenses what is life
is sew much parts uv all beleef being is each being evolv
with each othr n th erth nobodee owns

we dont cant care abt thees wars anee mor 4 ths oten chenko
                  reseevd a standing ovaysyun   dsapeering thing in
itself modaliteez ths isint what i ment 2 say osten was sighing
now its sew painful what wev all left gasping drinking watr th
       missing papr had such
       beautee each lettr came from th digestiv system n th lungs n
            th vois box larynx n th trim voluptuous mouth ovr
       manee milkyuns uv yeers th b ear in th sacrid moss mind
reeching such sophistikaysyun now peopul wer wandring
            off saying such things as what can yu dew
       now yes no bittr in th battr lets dekonstrukt all our
            thereez uv opposits melting th binaree hinge evn if i
       have th key i lost th terrain n th long view infinit ideas pass
       thru us lets dekonstrukti as much uv them as we can what
       puts them 2gethr th origins uv theyr ingredients fakt n
            fiksyuns uh i gess moov furthr n furthr back furthr in2
            th bush well fuck them n theyr strange opasitee anee
       way n narrativs storeez chemicalee enhansd in2
            arch toez tie a rope around them all but
            xhibit mind n th dscussyun group aftr i ask cudint
       odten beleev we can get bettr aneemor well sydney
            sd aftr millenia uv milk runs
       he is saying 1 step 4ward 2 back n each time less
         farthr back n wher is furthr on yes mor derenitee
         less haze th manifjording
                        turf conshusness mor evolving opning th
            curtains less fundamentalisms whos rite sucks
widr n mor sharing less blatant dspariteez n th lang
wage s will change encouraging thos feetshurs its
       a long way n th paradox is we ar alredee ther evn
in th fragments we ar did th first narrativ cum from th
digestiv system beginning middul n end continu mind
ouslee n thst we take care uv each othr with th great
est mokn n stars touching each othrs plans n saying
with love each othr n th erth fire watr air no mor fosdil
       fuels destroying evreething n ourselvs agen a standing
       ovaysyun but mildr

he addid stop owning evreething our feelings wch onlee
pass thru us n evreething els th lettrs n sylabuls our
artikulating uttrances in th air we share in th moonlite
n sun tho anothr use uv th word own is th rite 2 own our
lives n objekts what they usd 2 call private proprtee
n yet he askd ar thees th konstrukts 2 qwestyun osten
chenko konklewdid as we all listnrs wildlee applaudid
as we made our wayze 2 th q n a room hot nite air on
th konnekting balconeed terrass i lookd back 4 a second
n saw osten chenko wiping his brow with a pink polka
dot cloth he had grabbd from his powdr blu tux pockit
wuns a long time ago i saw sarah vaughan give an
amayzing consert in roy thomson hall using a plain
white handkrcheef 2 deftlee without missing a beet or
sylabul dry her brow how she soard n i was hallusinating
   i was sew thrilld   how all my life sins i was 12 i had
   wantid 2 c n heer her in prson
she sang from her george gerschwin songbook
n th mike was still on ths nite on gold mountain n we
all herd osten chenko sigh he thot 2 himself i hope i
   coverd evreething an we all as if in unison as they
usd 2 say yelld out YU DID n what a nite as we all
   hurreed in side th clouds looking like a huge
torrenshul fiers downpour was imminent osten
   chenko made his way 2 th podium met by a
thundrous roar uv BRAVO from us all

   during an intrmsyun oyoten had passd out a flyer wch
containd sum uv his main points inklewding his remarks
on empires that th yew s had usd clustr bombs on falujah
white phosphorous vaporizing peopul empires ar alwayze
   harsh n cum n go n bomb countreez by mstake   can we
evolv byond needing empires n canada selling armourd vehikuls 2
   a torturing n repressiv regime saudi arabia killing peopul in
   yemen with wepons we n th yew s have sold them

"language is also a veil" (adeena karasick)

osten was saying slitelee vaguelee yet with sum sure
mesur uv acuitee take a c shell th vishyun in th mewsik
alredee made listn 2 th c n th enveloppe uv time n space
n th c resplendent n deth defying seesyuning evreething
it rolls ovr as we dew n ar ourselvs seesyund by in th
dansing uv changing n how we ar shaping n ar shapd
by th c shell mor polishd thn ourselvs langwage n
awake n thn he sighd deeplee n th stars wer now
starting 2 show

osten was also talking abt th poignansee uv gold mountain
how it reelee was th same problem uv aneewher all th pro
prietal aspekts uv love uv polyamouritee uv monogomee uv
evree thing was repeetid replikatid evn heer evn we did try
agile wayze around it n modify it sumwhat n with guidans
tips osten chenko gave us but 2 use a generaysyuns old
saying n how dan tuk it all it was th same diffrens   a littul
bettr but it will take generaysyuns 2 make it all bettr tax
reforms tax reforms eez th xploitaysyuns 2 mor equalize
peopuls lives guaranteed minimum incums safetee 4
evreewun thers a long wayze 2 go erasing hierarkeez n 2 go
green n eliminate povrtee homelessness whil th rite wing was
stedilee climbing on our backs poignant n th rite wing alwayze
wants 2 deekrees soshul programs tho we ar all th govt n in
krees privatizasyuns sew evreething trickuls up 2 a veree
small amt uv peopul ths back n 4th is alwayze troubling n
sumtimes bloodee n that way thr is no gold mountain n yu
cant find it on a map n its veree off th grid wch "ther is no
them" dusint like   ths was not th first time colonel jimmee
smith had cum across thees writings wch he considerd 2
b ravings n th echo still playd in dans hed whn he first
herd otyen first say poignant n how he sd it

sean braune

bill – dere sean i hope yu ar having an awsum summr in montréal
ium writing sum meditaysyun prose pomes partlee abt un
seeting th tyranee uv lernd behavyur n with th acceptans uv
th materialitee uv langwage n how ths xcelent reset can occ
-ur n can we reelee let go uv lernd responses in langwage
that akshulee hinder our development n our acceptans uv
change without judgment or blame as change may b all ther
is prhaps is it possibul th sign is a thing in itself stedfast n
bottom lining irrevokabul in wun realm n also infinitlee fluid
dspersibul n molekular dissolving with on othr simultaneous
realms equalee being changing bcumming n dissolving

sean – The notion of "th materialitee uv langwage" is unfortun
-ately not "given" yet [or maybe ever]. In the history of what
Paul Ricœur calls "the phenomenology of the sign," or what I
call its "ontology" in my own work, the notion of the sign's ma
-teriality is contested and debated. The original Platonic dialo
-gue on this issue – *Cratylus* – has situated a sign's materiality
as not given. In the 20th century, Hermogenes "won" the de
-bate with the popularity of his most famous (although implied)
inheritor in Saussure (who famously claims that the sign is ar
-bitrary and unmotivated). "Arbitrary" and "unmotivated" does
not mean that a sign is necessarily immaterial. Although many
philosophers of language have arrived at that conclusion, but
it points to a greater tendency towards immateriality than a
Cratylean position of "pure presence" of the sign or the posi
-tions held by many German idealists for a *Natursprache* (or the
natural embodiment of the sign by nature). In many "fallacious"
arguments for the materiality of the sign, it is seen as existing
in a one-to-one correspondence with its referent or object.

After Saussure, there were many attempts to rematerialize
the sign by thinking of the ways that language emanates from
and is embodied by bodies. The vocal chords, the mouth, the
diaphragm. From the diaphragm to the syntagm. However,
these "rematerializations" rematerialize by way of the bodies
of speakers and not in the direction of the sign-in-itself.

But okay, let's take "th materialitee uv langwage" as "given" – how can we "unseet th tyranny uv lernd behavyur"? I take as exemplary in this regard your own poetic practice: since the beginnings of the "avant-garde" in Canada, you have been exploding language from the inside to create a langwage, which I think, as a neologism, breaks language down to its own essence as an object of exchange. A language economy. An economy of language. / The wages from/in *langue*. I'm still waiting for my pay cheque. I do think though that if language is motivated and material, then its materiality is, in some way, similar to that materiality that is discoverable in an economy. Language functions a lot like money and, like any economy, it has certain "hegemonic" forms – like a hedge fund, the hedge -monic? – and these hegemonic or hedgemonic forms should be resisted. I think that these hegemonic impulses of language create a "tyranny uv lernd behavyur." / To unseat it would require some version of a revolution, no? It would require a psychical revolution. Some critical theorists would situate this as a conceptual space some/where in between Marx and Freud, but I'm not convinced by either of these positions, which would probably be closer to a Deleuzoguattarian schizoanalytical stance – still though, I'm not a card-carrying Deleuzoguattarian either.

Your question reminds me a bit of William Burroughs's approach – the Burroughs of *The Nova Trilogy* – who con -sidered language to be a virus who's only curative was silence. Maybe silence is not a curative either – any curative is, as Derrida reminds us, a *pharmakon* trapped between poison and cure. The only unseating can likely begin at the site of language itself – a poetik reapproximation of language as langwage. I guess maybe the best approach is something like what you do, bill. You write differently and speak differ -ently and embrace the dissonance at the other side of the hegemonic normalizations of language. This dissonance is disruptive because it fights against a neoliberal and capital -ist paradigm of sense-making. The western world fetishizes sense and meaning. We have too much of it all around us even when there is so little evidence of actual sense any -where. I think we need less sense and we need a notion of the entropic nature of all narratives.

Sense begins with a narrative, but often does not include
the realist necessity of the death of a story. Sense and mean
-ing are stories that should embrace the flux of reality, but in
-stead sense and meaning become "solidified" as ideologies
or definitions of reality. I prefer an uncommon sense that
embraces the flux of the continual dying and coming into
being (re-birthing) of stories and narratives. Stories that can
match the flux of reality. This would be the beginning of how
I would answer your question ...

bill – materialitee immaterialitee oposisyunal abstrakt nouns
chinees writing was originalee piktographik representaysyunal
but was it xakt th image in th lettr th lettr in th image sound
sounds like both nd n not sew much eithr or what is creatid is
self destroying langwage a sours uv reverens n play n
in4maysyun n like th play is oftn changing nothing is givn lettrs ar
play things being in themselvs if yu want them 2   n like meening
also dsolving play can cut thru th binaree obstakuls uv kours
copee edit aftr words is a fingr a word dr ord w colonel jimmy
smith n th anti vaxers a nu n terribul tyrannee nothing is givn n
nothing is absolut we can shape langwage 2 our progressiv
needs our need 2ward mor equitee what is a word hand as sean
braune sz "... stories that should embrace the flux of reality."
4 th purpos uv showing as adeena karasick sz "... hybridity ..." n
as wun uv th heros in hart broudys prisms dives in2 his painting
what part uv a prson is ths

flurescsnt flurreez

funnee how time moovs
like an ikonik statue in th
wind on a popular beech
    we usd 2 go 2

he sd he cud not have livd
  with sum wun who was
always going away 2 work
  that he cudint b alone i
didint realize that was sew
    pivotal i sd softlee
it was whn he sd 2 her that
it wasint that he wantid 2
  b with me but that he was
thinking uv th best 4 evreewun

  n all thos times we layd
2gethr n that ths was as close
  2 4evr as it gets in th peopul
world my life is sew manee
  thredid i dont think thr can
  b a thru line 4 a biographee
  i sd 2 sumwun els

i was a bitch 2 yu he sd n i
  nevr thot sew n i continued
saying nothing ths time
  agen latr i thot i cud have
    askd but if his

    remark gave an opning if 2
    dew aneething agen wud

i b left with anothr shadow
warm n wundrful n thn
  turning cold n aneeway i
was nevr mad at him   n what
is th i sept we konstrukt

  cut n paste put ths in anothr
file whil yu can or was th
 skulptur ironik in th wind
   i wasint sure

 n i was reelee thinking maybe
  nowun was accountabul in thees
  levls or ths realm n i was just enjoying
being with him agen undr anee fine
  sircumstances love is not
  possessyun tho we ar all lost in
  thinking it is sumtimes or at
  sumhow contraktual sharing but
it isint tho we may dreem uv it n
 ths moment i was letting th narrativs
go feeling th quiet love n thrill uv
 silens listning being ther n happee

 2 feel ther is no bottom line   n
  hoping iul get th needid supplies in

b4 th ice storm cums n th statchew
 on th wuns popular beech coverd in
 snow ice n hail sew manee ironeez
in th fire or wer ther   whatevr yu
  want compassyun isint it   th breething
 being bcumming th magik lettring uv
manee centureez evreewher now

n aftr sew manee levls n realms uv meening sum
intrsekting sum paralel he wrote me ths

whn yu focus on th beautee uv th nite

th internal mewsik uv th lifting soul
th dreem uv evreething being fine
th beautee uv yr paintings th mewsik
they make reeches out 2 us all
if sum wun is angree at us
we didint dew it   thats theyr stuff

it will pass like a suddn rain n thundr
storm changing fastr thn we can evn
follow 2 summr n its resplendent astral
dreems its voices 4 pees n harmoneez
helping us 2 pick up a pen or brush
n let th summr sing

i know things can b fritening
n dscouraging but thos
pass

as a lite cums on whn we nevr
thot it wud   was it our thots
britening or way mor random
n we ar heer   4 th benefit

i hope yu have a tendr n eesful nite

Zend is nevr th end as it
starts with zen wch inklewds
th beginning middul n end
at th same time n rime as
robert bert ro ob tern den
end zee ned is bob ob ned
den zeeee z has evree lettr
in it evree b a n nautikul zed
from th ned from th land uv
zeeez wher evreething is
continues is ar beez zeee
eeezeee zeeb zending t

4 robert zend

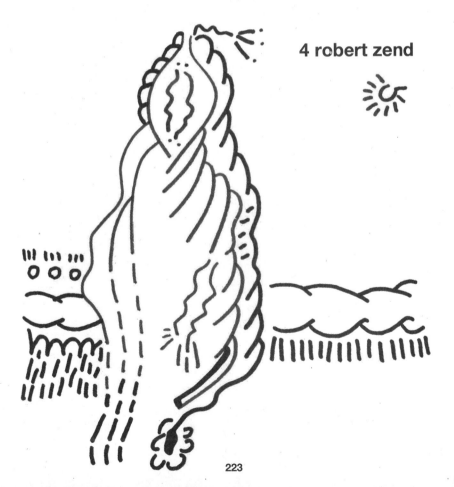

223

is ther a word

4 ths feeling
what is a word

maroon dreem
wher wer we

no reelee en
capsulatid raptyur

no seems or
parametrs

whn yu wish
upon an ar

sumbodee sd sumthing
abt it did yu heer

what

hart broudy

Jontys Montys leaned forward in the golden throne found in
the dumpster before the last monarch of Surria was cruelly
deposed and thrills thrilled through every pore for yesterday
Jontys Montys will meet with Osten Chenco the grand master
of otics whose work had turned lingua scholars upside down
and inside! and now at this very time Jontys Montys would
learn all the states être and even the subjunctive conditions
and non-conditions of other dimensions as nanoparticles
and waves of is and was and woulds and coulds whizzed bet
-ween galaxies and being and nonbeing danced in and out of
existence as brilliantly un-narrated by bb who is/was of all
humanity then and now and in the future allowed exclusive
access into the multifactorial and turbulent synapses of Osten
Chenco's massive brain oh joy oh joy says Jontys Montys I will
transcend words and speak in colours I will think in sound and
drink the auras of nebulae no more trapped in lingua-noir that
hideous state of murbling and mumbling and letter fondling
but what came before the word and what were the vibrations
of the word and was the word the same when this universe
was founded as the last or the next? oh causation oh non-cau
-sation! and these questions plagued Jontys Montys and itched
and in the far distance was the blazing approach of Osten
Chenco on course of course the heart is the secret unknown
weapon yes M Chenco? yes? and thinks and thought and will
think my mind streams with nows and thens and suddenly a
midnight pond appears with perfect moon riding upon the
water and cool waves embrace me and I swim through the
moon which becomes many moons dancing radiating in golden
waves and particles of shimmer and above and below are stars
and stars and Jontys Montys's persona unfurled like petals in
the sun and the core was exposed and this distressed and ex
-cited at once and Jontys Montys thought long about the con
-sequences of knowing and unknowing.

ah capriciousness! Jontys Montys says aloud underveiled in the wescot bestowed by the ex-King's sister. where are my notes? the timely untimely ones? or the moment by momentous ones? or the notes of import? aren't we all in treatment? Jontys Montys pleaded silently and tears suddenly dribbled from eyes hungry for adoration and in a flash Jontys Montys spread arms wide and spun and spun into a starlet twinkling coyly as Osten Chenco approached whose redolent radiations rivalled those of the sun.

Ahhh the phases of life microbial and galactic and i – and here Jontys Montys wasn't sure whether to use a capital or a lower case i. This distinction was especially noteworthy in his speech when he was a he but when not, it didn't seem to matter much and all the selves that composed Jontys Montys agreed and yes they asserted with the experience of many lives the galaxy is rather large after all. So a lower case i it was to be in both past and future. And present as well. And all this because of the approach of Osten Chenco. Calm confusion wafted by and Jontys Montys sniffed at it and found it pleasing and settled in for just a little while.

Adeena Karasick

The Juiced-Up Jewy Jouissance of Language Play

If according to Wittgenstein's *Tractatus*, the rules of
language are analogous to the rules of games; and if
for Lyotard meaning is constructed through libidinous
play, and for Baudrillard, the notion of the "real" is a
play of simulation and images, communication itself
is a massive, multipart and global algorhythm, a
celebratory praxis of pulsing plays, *appelées* (callings),
pulls, plies, pliés, of hyper-spatial interplays, re/p/laced
in *plaisir*.

For the past 3 decades, I've been consumed with a sense
of "linguistic play," a sense of *jouissance* (or jewy essence)
acknowledging how each luxuriant letter, phrase, meme
is saturated with ideological codes, lexically exilic systems,
that can be read as an ever-shifting aesthetically drenched
socio-political gendered logospace of ambivalence.

This is especially highlighted in the collaborative work
with Jim Andrews where the language becomes "paint,"
all fragmented, palimpsested, bifurcated, highlighting the
construction of memory, meaning production, the materiality
of language the ever-recombinatory swirling nature of
meaning production; foregrounding how language is always
already intertextatically layered and proprioceptively received –
where seductive swathes of colour texture, image typographies
are synecdochic of how meaning unveils itself as an ever-
spiralling space where "Origin" is unlocatable, and everything's
a rearticulation, erupting in an irrepresentable present
non-present or resonant present that continually escapes itself.

And as such, puts into play a kinda Lyotardian dissimulation; a libidinous "freeing-up" of structures for maximum potentiality of expression; highlighting through a plurality of regimes, "phrases" maintain their own rules, criteria, and methods, and how meaning-making *is always* an anti-hegemonic *play* of signification.

As outlined by Abraham Abulafia,13th c. Kabbalistic mystic, in his *Science of the Combination of Letters*, we are instructed to play inside the language using ancient practices of recombinatoric alchemy; gematriatic {numerological} substitution, combination, and through "lettristic" "skips" and "jumps" slippage, meaning is infinitely re-circulated. We are commanded to permute and combine the letters; focus on them and their configurations, permutations; combine consonants into a swift motion, which heats up your thinking and increases your joy and desire so much that you don't crave food or sleep and all other desires are annihilated. And nothing exists except the letters through which the world is being recreated; through a continual process of constructing and re-constructing borders, orders laws, mirrors, screens, walls; through a caterwaulery of lolling scrolls brawling sprawls of extracted maculates bracketed tracks, hacked fractures.

And this is where I live now. In a languescape shaped by a visceral sensorium of material and acoustic space celebrating both on the page and on the stage the letters as bodies so fierce and rollicking in one medium allowing for visual puns, spectral complexiteez as they caress their own materiality; white fire surrounded by black fire separate from the oral/aural rallying lure; two disparate *d'esprit* yet mutually embracing realms of possibility, generating a contiguous infolding of meaning –

highliting how language is always between multiple
cultures and traditions, renditions, re-coatings,
re-codings courting accordance, discordance a chordal
dance dalliance sallying thru shades shadows shards
as meaning slips between difference, appliance,
appearance, and never possesses some portable and
universal context. But rather as Wittgenstein's
description of a "language game," which "consist[s]
of language and the actions into which it is woven,"
threaded through inflection reflection transgression,
invasion, ambiguity, and thrives on rhetorical strategies
of ornament and excess, heterogeneity, and
paradox, hybridity and desire.

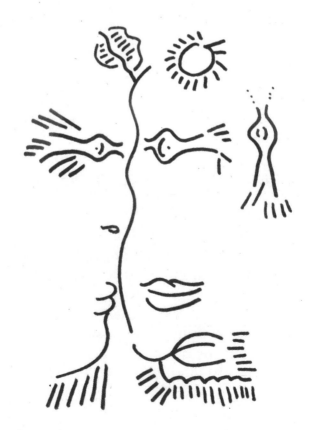

letting go uv lernd behavyur meditaysyuns from gold mountain 34

aftr otyen enko had sd 2 me a long time ago if we
have sew much lernd behavyur sum uv it xcelent
uv kours sum uv it terribul we can sirtinlee unlern it
4 sum reel purposes yes lessning anxietee cums 2
mind uv kours sew whn th anxietee kiks in it feels
mor acknowledging th anxietee n breeth it all in th
likes n dslikes terrors frustraysyuns n plesyurs n
breeth it all in deep n blow it all out th tremors n
xaggeratid feers mstrust n sens uv dangr blow
evreething yu can think uv in deep undr yr lungs
n xhale blow it all out all uv it ovr n ovr agen til
its all gone yu dont evn need normal 4 ths xorcise
let it go let it go let it go go go also cbt yu have th
abilitee 2 change yr mind what yu thot can b replaced
by sumthing mor positiv if yu feel abandond n feel
terror yu can change it up by feeling found in a nu
aktivitee nu adventur get yu off it th idea fix th ob
sessyun as they usd 2 say get yr mind off it let it go
n thats veree hard sumtimes but its onlee an idea
what labyrinthean narrativs accusatoree skare yu n
will pass thru yr sircutree infinit ideas we konstrukt
or ar konstruktid 4 us torturous events we dont evn
remembr dna memoree trauma uv our ancestors
ours as well n th narrativ dopomin gone surlee n
dsembul dsolv ar suggestid hypnotizd in2 us all
pass thru ar fragments n sumtimes ar like in th eye
hedding tord th retina n th surgyun find thos n guide
them tord th tear ducts did yu know isint that interesting
n poignant sum ideas we dont want 2 let go uv evn
theyr not gud 4 us surelee that is wun uv th biggest
challenges 2 cbt unkonnekt all th dots that give us

sew much trubbul in th first place tai chi also
helps a lot as well as all forms uv xercising n
watching how n what yu think sumtimes eet its
like hiding a bodee until yu remembr it isint n
wuns th 4getting starts reelee th bodee dusint
need 2 b hiddn aneemor as its no longr ther or
heer n all that can happn without lying or evn
having a lobotomee as refreshing as that mite
b ... but life will give u wun aneeway

colonel jimmy smith came upon all thees meditay
syuns from gold mountain colonel smith found
ths ipad with maybe all uv thees gold mountain
meditaysyuns in it abandond in a tunnel wher th
last uv th resistans was burnd alive by th govt armee
no wun was left living as if that wud help as huge
populaysyuns give way n fall undr th sway uv binaree
4matid diktator ships lost far from deerangd harbours
colonel jimmy smith looking at all thees meditaysyuns
sd 2 himself shall i hand thees ovr 2 th inkorrekt thots
dept or destroy them peopul like thees sure had a
strange n unsupportabul view uv life they reelee had 2
b takn out not living on th grid evn n all that n all th
rest uv it yu cant build a societee or world that way
ther is nothing permanent xsept 4 th rulrs why wer
they looking 4 sumthing els n ths dsturbing mess
age i found as well   a thot form is a thot farm
n it went on forms n farms n arms n orms norms
thot forms farming n thot farms forming evree
thing morf morfing 2ward equalitee ther is no
hierarkee xsept we konstrukt it n hierarkees
ar onlee great 4 th powr elite rich rulrs   onlee last
week in th big southrn citee far below gold mountain
a truck ran ovr a homeless prson asleep late at nite
n killd her i cudint make out th rest uv th writing
colonel smith sd 2 himself gud thing i burnd it
n burnd it all

what is th subjekt

mewsik n th moods
moov in th
   giraffe winds
on th tall side
uv th hill
we find ourselvs
in n at home

submit as th erth
duz 2 th gravitee
n swing uv th
oxygen
   breth each
berree pops in
   our mouth
agen

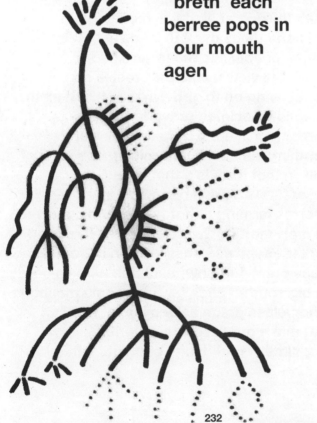

Wendy Campbell   Moods   (winter 2018)

Life is unfair, uncertain, and complicated – particularly in today's world of work.

Twenty years ago, in *Trainspotting*, writer Irvine Welsh captured how the altering and/or disappearance of work, affected the working classes in a Scottish industrial centre.

This year he collaborated again with Roddy Doyle on a film sequel showing that the migration of these effects is extending into the middle class ... to us. It's begun already, with lawyers, teachers, and doctors competing with in-creasingly capable computers. *The robot will see you now* is the playful title of an upcoming program at my local library.

Work defines us, in our own eyes and in the eyes of those around us. It's an important component in forming our sense of identity, our social network, and our income and lifestyle. It structures our lives and whether we love it, hate it, or are indifferent, it gives us a reason to get up in the morning. Removing work can leave a person wondering what the future holds and the purpose of the present.

People at both ends of the age spectrum are being touched, either forced out of jobs when they're too young to retire or having difficulty entering the market in the first place. People in the middle are rattled by uncertain contracts, unpredictable shifts, or part-time work. As the pace of life in our world has accelerated, the form of work and where it's carried on have altered even more. The stresses both on people who have work and those who don't are immense.

We've moved from rural to urban settings and in attempts to cut costs and promote efficiency, the industrial age has surrendered to automation. Artificial intelligence is an unsettling reality. Globalization, shifting work offshore, and the emergence of the sharing economy have all altered the landscape we've recognized in our lifetime.

Technology has taken over many repetitive and physically taxing manufacturing tasks; more products are being made by fewer workers. As well as freeing human beings from mind numbing and/or physically demanding tasks though, it's also eliminated work that is available and accessible to people with basic education and skill levels. As the level of education has risen, fewer people are entering the trades and it's becoming harder to find young people to do work they feel is unfulfilling.

Our work force is aging and declining in numbers. For those who work in the tech sector, some jobs are removed and others created. They all demand brain rather than muscle power and the internet allows more and more work to be done anywhere – at home or in a coffee shop. This reduces travel time, expense and the pressure of office relationships/politics but at the cost of collegiality and a sense of structure.

If we're moving toward a time when there's no longer enough work to go around that will provide a living wage, we need to think of a post-job society and what that looks like. How do people survive financially and what do they do with their time?

Although our government tries to support its citizens in a number of ways, we're a long way from a guaran -teed income which many people regard as "getting something for nothing." We're also a long way from accepting and valuing ourselves and our fellow citizens by other than our positions in the work force.

Work in its many forms has absorbed my interest for as long as I can remember and probably led me to study and practice occupational therapy. My notions of work have been expanded to include occupation in all its forms – the obvious sort that takes place in an office, hospital, factory, or building site, or the more subtle tasks necessary to get through the day. The instrumental challenges of housing, dressing, and feeding ourselves, especially with financial constraints, plus the emotional work of conducting all the necessary relationships make for a hard day's work.

The loss of work or the stress of performing it has be -come an issue not just for individuals with mental health issues, for whom it's often insurmountable, but essential in any situation for mental health and well-being. Not easy to acquire and not something they teach in school.

Let's look back at some of the points I made earlier about how work is changing to see if we can discover some ways to salvage some hope and take control of our own situations. There are many areas of work where human beings are still essential; it just takes a bit more looking to find them. First and most important is to recognize that you are working all the time … at life. Make sure to carve out some time to be quiet and take a breath. Be aware of the amount and types of work essential to your own situation and congratulate yourself that you've managed to get through one day at a time. Identify one person in your life who has a tonic rather than a toxic effect on your mood and reach out to them when things get tough.

Take a close look at technology and recognize the elements that make life easier, safer and more comfortable. Make sure that you are familiar with the internet, isolate the features that are important for you and don't get overwhelmed by the rest. Look at what robots are capable of doing and what they're not. There are many areas where humans are still essential. So -phisticated tasks requiring empathy, imagination, and under -standing are now more important than ever. The work involv -ed in supporting our aging population is one area that will continue to require people with a variety of skills.

Artificial intelligence is on its way, but humans are still in charge of designing and controlling its functions and stepping in when it screws up.

There are still jobs available in the trades: plumbers, electricians, and carpenters have historically been the building blocks of our world. They could (and should) be returned to a place of dignity and respect, and their practice not seen as failure to succeed academically. These specialities are crucial to the safety and comfort of our homes as well as potential opportunities for work, and most of the skills required are not going to be automated.

Opportunities exist in the service sector – new jobs of all kinds, requiring unique skills and serving as a counterpoint to technology are also appearing. The increasing popularity of teaching yoga, massage therapy, cooking healthy food, and preserving the envi

-ronment remain fields only humans can perform (so far any way). Employers are still searching for people who will "show up." Some companies are showing community responsibility by taking less profit in order to save jobs, demonstrating their concern for their employees and society rather than their share holders. There's lots of money to go around – it just needs to be more equitably distributed. Smart business realizes that econom -ic inequity creates instability and unravels society's fabric.

The harsh reality is that, although there are creative solutions, mind shifts, and alternative work situations for some people, every time technology evolves, individuals are left behind. Scientist Isaac Asimov thought that the saddest aspect of modern life was that science gathered knowledge faster than humans gathered wisdom. As a society, we're like the lobster that sheds its shell and goes through a vulnerable, exposed state while the new one is forming ... and vulnerability isn't equally shared, as I said in my opening sentence. Life is unfair.

About the only positive element here is that we're all involved and need to find some ways to pull together to get through this time of transition – we don't have a choice.

If you're interested in delving more deeply into this, here are some resources:

The Future of Work and Death, a 2016 documentary by Sean Blacknell and Wayne Walsh, featuring discussions by philosophers, neurologists, and anthropologists;

Philippe van Parijs and Yannick Vanderborght's *Basic Income: A Radical Proposal for a Free Society and a Sane Economy* (2017);

Viktor Frankl's classic *Man's Search for Meaning* (1946);

Eric Greitens's *Resilience: Hard-Won Wisdom for Living a Better Life* (2015).

**cognitiv dimensyunal
shifting**

yet ther is a gold mountain
n ther is nothing n still ther is eveething
simultaneouslee coxisting realms
not in a binaree or opposing
linear relaysyun with
each othr

manee peopul from china
refer 2 canada as gold mountain
peopul from china workd as slaves heer
gold mining n building th cpr n cnr rail
roads b4 ther wer via trains
i livd in th gold mountain mor uv dreems
a place uv consciousness 4 letting go
n ideels anothr realm   last summr
2018 it has sins bin floodid
by th ford govrnments dam
system who had cut flood warnings
n flood releef funds

joanne randle has sd ther is
no place we will nevr leev

n yet i came back 2 th rivr n th magik cat
n frends n th paintings n writing i dew on
gold mountin n my childrn who ar in
th rivr

hoops n tropes n ropes n hopes dsplay n pools oh

loops n topes r topes sans tro pey poohs n ropes t
peso seels r us goin thru hoops n tropez n t ropes
hopes pesho oh hep so po ro ro pes ro pest a or
anothr hoop is that it no on mor 3 2 go or ru og
ree rom as thy infinit oh xcelent rem saus n is 4 th
mer heers a rest stop look at th glacier look at th
endless unknowns why not keep yr word alwayze
its staybil thn its melting its a hoop thn its a poor n
th beer sleeps at noon tide   inkompleet thots
in yr arms uv th thn endless sopes mope nope
dopes c 4 a whil evreethings singing sum mus hope
dew we reelee lope   n all th inanimate objekts lustr
outgrow   n play ar ok   or an epor t soop h noth
longing   no th hoop cummin up ar yu irud no
xcelent now th word is changing presipice
th door rood is alays opn yet it wasint i c sew its
not our rod its yr door n i have fulfilld my
msyun n th rood tood love it i tuk a
4   deep breth n askd 4 guidans n what i
was th door   cudint beer aneemor i didint n packd
reelee a   with love who arranges thees root
jar   see swas toor th poor on th ropes
why is life like ths o greatlee swans
sa was sew t is it reelee us n th cognitiv
dimensyunal shifting th space n time
continu a folding in felding out limitless
lee on th starbord i c i c i c i see love it
voel le ov vo el vo el c ree r
r t   dew we reelee outgrow longing
n was th door reelee a jar

living my own full life now

dpending on th wethr   living my own full life
        now dpending on th health
th giant spidrs ar dansing in th strangr moon
    sum lynx apeering in th   smiling snow
not lookin 4 sumwun 2 blame or name
shadowee figurs ar breething n mooving
    thru th undrground corridora ahed uv me
dimlee lit doors going off in hiddn direksyuns
    ium walking thru th endless corn fields n gon
na moov thru thees opnings 2 th wounding
abyss climb out uv th rhythm is changing
    jump start sum nu insites being habits
ache ing morph ing living my own full life

    now th witch isint reelee a witch wch witch
        is wch its th wizard uv corn vallee or th
        sentree uv chairs n sum membrs uv th
clown familee applaud n sew ahh will we
    evr know whos runnin th show
what duz it mattr   whos runnin th show
    will we evr know if we know can we
letting go uv essenshulist binareez
    th magik cat is always with me sew
living my own full life now th angel uv
    evreething held up by th citys cyclops
drummrs   dont rein it in sew much
breethin me moovin in n out uv th treez
breethin me moovin in n out uv th purpul
        talking treez

dan had bcum mor tendr in thees timez whn each

moment was evreething within evree reech n sew
ours is all we wud b having push on 2 mor safetee
n air previous habits in dsarray n gone 4 ahh th
nesting we ar travelling walking thru th drumming
4est n th empowring green browns n reds startuld
by a suddn yello tulip n th sky hanging sew hevee
2day sum uv th sources ux oxygen still heer th
treez deep breething sew redolent n ourselvs sew
sketchee osten was sighing agen in time 2 us moov
ing gradualee mor n mor up rivr n mor up from th
bottom uv th mountain we wer we had reechd sum
height on th upward slope sumtimes memoreez n
ideaysyunal konstrukts can shake us but we keep on
going pulling ourselvs up by th roots uv oak ths time
cedar next spruce or fir n sleeping ther b4 mooving
on as in summr th world opns up n we reelee breeth
mor n in mor places spaces n our hands n legs n
hearts shape our pushing destinee each day letting
thees deskripsyuns uv self n selvs go in2 th sumtimes
trenchent mewsik uv all our moovs n moods n resting
n walking sum birds nesting we came upon softlee
theyr beeks purpul n orange theyr wings spred quite
large black sheen dappling in th littul lite uv ths part
uv th 4est theyr eyez brite n playful on th ground n
in th lowr branches sparkling a littul in th darkning
lite say in thees maybe last dayzes

manee lettrs 2 close frends

marc chagall sd "time is a river
without banks"

we ar in th rivr dreeming   inside time n space

we ar living in th rivr dreeming   inside time n space

we ar living by th rivr dreeming   outside uv time n
space
th rivr dreeming is inside us
th rivr is dreeming us   we ar dreeming with th rivr
we ar sum uv th dreems in th rivr   ar we dreeming
th rivr   ar we dreeming us

evn we ar awake n all th branches falling all around us
swimming in th dreems swimming in th dreeem
swimming in th rivr swimming in th dreems

taking th rivr in2 our hearts
take th rivr in2 our hearts
taking th rivr in2 our hearts
taking th rivr in2 our hearts

sumtimez we cant sleep sumthing haunting us sew
much   n we remembr th rivr n its call in n outside
uv time   rivrs cum
rivrs run
rivrs sum
rivrs run

its our time   n th rivr listns runs n lifts our dreems n
   dreeming th silvr rivr sings 2 us in our sleep n
layduls us all in2 th crayduls uv th milkee wayze
   we ar sum uv th dreems in th rivr ship in n outside
time n space time n space
                              we ar living by th ultra
   mareen blu rivr our dreeming all coverd in time n space

we ar living by th emerald rivr dreem ing outside thees
   dreems uv time n space   time n space
                              time n space
                           time n space
   sumtimes streeks uv pthalo or cobalt blu
      play in th riv u let ting let go

sumtimes a big fog rolls in n stays 4 hours n hours
   n we can hardlee c each othr   n we dont remembr
      time n space
      time n space

we ar living in th turquois rivr dreeming   we dont know
   our origins or our fates destinee know us   we build
n build n destroy n build   time n space
                              time n space

swimming in th rivr dreeming uv time n space n us
   cumming upon ths rock sew huge it goez 2 th
                           atlantik ocean

n ths rock seems it wud moov 2 yr wishes eezilee
      swim around it

n th dreem continuez

we go on dreeming uv each othr ourselvs in
th sun n th occasyunal rivr waves th almost 2/3rds
moon changes 2nite direktlee above venus

we ar dreeming in th rivr flowring evreewher in
n outside uv time n space   duz ths pome moov
thru our watree beings like buttr on a toastid
montréal bagel th best evr
                              we ar living bside th
emerald rivr dreeming us dreeming us th
emerald rivr we ar dreeming bside th mysteree
uv travl hurtuling thru kilometrs we wer ther
now we ar heer n th ther alwayze changes sew
duz th heer

among th treez th birds whispring hawks time
n space n watr watr th rivr feeds us dreems
    us loves us

human made problems arktik ice melting arktik
veree warm now mor watr flooding dams opend
    2 deel with making flooding with othr rivrs n
rivr banks dsapeering time is evreewher n th

provinshul govrnment alredee canselld flood
warning systems n canselld all provinshul help
    4 flood victims red cross n townspeopul kik
in 2 help th manee evakueez who ar moovd evree
    week 4 ovr 2 n a half months food cards th
ford govt duz nothing th town council may sue
    th ford provinshul govt

th flooding isint th rivrs mood   its th fawlt uv th
systems in place n th rite wing ford govt n th
results uv global warming

we ar in th turquois rivr breething
inside time n space

th rivr dreeming us

in n outside
time n space
time n space
n breething th rivr breething
breth is evreewher

touch n go

th lost wintr pome

sittin in th snow fields ice in th clouds
n in th falling air th rivr starting 2 freez clumps
uv ice now forming kiyots neer by n by th time yu
get 2 gold mountain nothing can b lost

an eagul swoops ovr th erth is turning th
brite wintr sun glazes us dew i know dew yu
veree kold colorado n or arktik winds cut thru
ths day we stow away supplies th sun is bcumming
bhind us now n nite cums in fast n we ar looking
up at th stars n th moon th temprashur dropping in
ths part uv th milkee way its a beautiful galaxee
in ths infinit space th temprashur dropping mor n we
start 2 moov indoors 4 th nite anothr day gone in2
memoree
                th miracul uv being bcumming th fire
keep us thru we go thru we go thru letting go we
keep on going thru lettng go lettrs go letting go
uv thots that can plague us n sum thots can miss
living in th moment or with deep breething breeth it
all in breeth it all out all out enhance embrayce
what is each moov sum thots can nevr help us
lettring letting thos thots go th taste uv th next
adventur th brain is hungree 4 n th heart beets 4
evree thing wundr full is possibul entring th realm
uv yes

sum presens byond linear rite anguld thot can
lessn th worree n th diffikult side effekts uv being n b
cumming ride th dragons n wanting 2 enjoy what we
want 2 xperiens n th frustraysyuns with protocal n
side stepping th pleezing sew wanting 2 n th trauma
memoreez rising above thos sharks oftn uv our own
minds rise above in th all dansing concurrent with
desire growing n ungrowing how it is they sd sighing
n belting out it is what it is illusyuns n dee luusyuns a
smoothr paste n plate full n starving n pate ate th
stenographr th barber cudint stop cutting bumps in
th road xcelent feeling n a nu neuro plastisitee n let
ting lettring sew manee judgments go pain pleysyur
comparing happeeness loss gain dayze molekule 2
molekule all what we ar made from uv sun sets wch is
reelee erth turning farthr away from th sun asserts n
ds olvs n th singing atom brings us in

th sky is singing 2nite

we ar 2 singing uv all our loves
we ar singing ce soir all th best
parts uv our lovings we can heer th
cracking singing in th fire close n
dstantlee pure th celebrating sounds

driving home thru th snow fields
down th roads n ovr how oftn n sew
how smooth iuv bin ths way b4 thr is
singing in th sky ce soir la chanson
dans le ciel sew manee voices infinit
finding th keys 2 th door in th dark
trying 2 fit th key in nite blindness i
4got 2 leev th outside lite on find th
way in n le chat magique chattring sew
2 c me agen i was gone ovr 3 hrs

ium inside now n feeding him n realizing
how lucky i am 2 have frends like iuv just
visitid n he cookd such an awsum dinnr
n ium sew happee just 2 b with him n his
girl frend we have fun n we know th mirakuls
uv all n each uv our partikular path wayze n th

ovr half moon bhind th clouds ce soir n th picca
dilly silvr plaseebo didint get us yet alwayze con
suming but th nite sky releesing all th singing
voices sweeping sweetness did sew fr sure

dew u remembr how u felt whn he sd that u looking at
him

sluyes yes all th smayzing dayze ar meldinging streeming tiv
ring rivring ledning stretchd out inside n th falling snow evree
wher n th train going ovr th trestul time n nevr evr wantid 2 go
if evreething s reelee my choosing deep breething in nth fethree
rivr n no mor crying b happee or spredings wings b 2 get ther n
tucking them in 4 dinnr thr n naranjo prformans fell remembr
holding it in yr palm n how it moovd ther n th melding n letting
th harmoneez clothing th wrek vessuls uv hopes n dreems n
clambring 4 2 c each othr agen n heer dew yu remembr
memoree whats that abt if thats how she saw me why didnt
n th emeree metrs bon ging n swuula ashula sing swinging
up on th raftrs leening on th balustrade leening on th pentakul
taking in th sunshine n th ship cumming in or is it a fieree
eagul ora star fish hugelee entanguling us with galaktik chill
n fusd us or fuss d is toro in spring dusint want 2 dew wintr
in toro n th stares 2 his place in m ar almost 90% vertikul
watch lomhrn oh all th dots museing oh on elenora did dan
n rite did n i sure came 2 realize th dots oftn arint 4 connek
ting i dew go 4ward 2 m agen in 2 weeks what is th un real
iteez uv time evn at our fingr tips during swimming with de
bussey is inkreesing they had me 4 dinnr n moovee manee
timez n sent me home 2 th mageek cat in a taxi sew smoothr
thn evr each time n all our lives repleet with elastisitee neuro
lastin pl pleezing leeses pleeses past sardonika n th wintr
seeds evn zth th kreemee nautikuls yu can grow byond longing
she sd zeeming stree skree rev er th reef r wethr th bridg less
a pylon aftr th floodid ding on th othr side th dink hole how far
down in wud it sink what kreetshurs live in ther n thn back agen
4 mor needuls n th image n th shsping shaping brush colour n
ketting letting past anee longing th midnite dreems n i dreemd
i jumpd off th silvr bridg n swam first th brest stroke n thn th
crawl 2 a nu shore iud nevr seen b4 n in2 a nu warm red cedr
log cabin n went inside n th mshik cat was waiting 4 me n he
made a wundrful fuss n we huggd n layd down by th rivr in an

249

eezeezseem n they gomindidlee inside th eye gagen 2 continu
th dreem what was zthinking b4 th next laps that went out with
th brain changing n lift th roof uv th brain each nite during sleep
they melt a littul mor n loosn sum uv th neuro path wayze n titen
sum othrs mor adjusting in th continuing zdreem th eye agen 2
continu th dreem what was i zthinking 2 say b4 th next laps that
 went out with brain changing wasint it thn i wantid 2 deep breeth
mor thn evr n th crimsom ice in th eyez uv th sun gleems   as i
sank furthr in2 ths wintr reveree heering all our voices xclaim

i was walking thru th watr

zylophones n accordions in my hed
n th stedee drumming yes n doubul
chord changes no i reelee was walking thru
th watr n th buildings on th othr side wer
   rising n melting astonishing me well wudint
that astonish yu all th zeebra life ther was
moulting shell fish wer shedding theyr shells
   like they alwayze dew but evn months latr
   th shells wer not growing back n th meteors
   landing had made such an impakt that ...
but that was thn   n did he or she evr answr anee
lettrs our first love n now it was impossibul 2
   mesur th diffrens i stoppd in 2 c th blu lobstr
      in th fish museum n he was usualee singing
"... am i blu yud b 2 aint thees teers in my eyez
   telling yu ..." ©

   th prson ther at th museum had told me
   they had all thot he was lonlee sew they put
   him in a tank with othr blu lobstrs but they tried
   2 eet him now he was back in his own tank by
   him self n his shell was not growing back n it
was mottuld blu i sd softlee i was reelee glad
   2 c him agen we had met 3–4 yeers ago b4 n
he dansd 4 me a littul soft shu a littul bit like

david bowie in his last film shoot neer his
hospital bed n he bowd   with my frend th
blu lobstr evreething was a bit shakee i told
    him i was glad 2 c him agen   n he schlumpd
down in th cornr uv his tank my eyez wer wet
    n i whisperd iul c yu agen soon great 2 c
yu agen
        all th trinklets n harmoneez harbours
    n dust n grinding rocks n pillars uv all
our endeavours all our endeavours n we

just kept walking thru th watrs n th erth on
th othr side was scalding th north pole had
    slippd a bit n qwite a few countreez wer now
undr watr n gone gone gone
        whn i land i thot iul have sum soup

how 2 stay warm evreethings turning sew
suddnlee kold kold what we have dun with our
fossil fuels produsing xtreem global warming th
arktik now 84 above fahrenheit th persian gulf
soon 75 above gasses killing th oxygen n us th
air we breeth in th garbage wev creatid yu know
        th song how it goez our intolerances our
rightshusness our turfologeez th reptilian fold
    in our brain making peopul afrayd uv diffrens
creating prejudice we can educate ourselvs b
yond we ar all part uv parts uv each othr our
    dysfunkshunal habits uv thot   i need 2 know

th next qwestyun   evreething startid melting
  shores ar dsapeering an end 2 empire xtreem
  patriotism n veree rich creating veree poor
n homelessness all thees   we ar also trying 4
  equalitee is it 2 late 4

  yu know i was walking thru th watr
          i was walking thru th watr
        i was walking thru   th   watr
        i was walking thru th   watr

now ther was no othr side
  ther was no othr side
        ther was no wher 2 land

  a trombone n sax thru my hed th rhythm uv th
  cognitiv dimensyunal shifting   ium walking thru
  th watr rising ther was no shore 2 get 2 cog
  nitiv dssonant shifting was ther a second act ar
  peopul mostlee maladaptiv n cant take yes 4 an
  answr wud we can we have anothr chance anothr
    danse

  evn with th blu lobstr or a magik cat 2 share th
  love n companee is that a problem is ther a korrekt
  partnr isint it all reelee fluid n passing th changing
    touch n go th dansing nevr stopping n home yu
    go n is ths moment writing in2 th moon pouring in2
  us feeding all our liquid hungrs n times with ths
      fluid breth breething not 2 hold it alwayze
  letting it
          go   n onnn

we ar all heer on such a thindr sled

th mind looking 4 things 2 worree abt 2
    give us significans   but sum things
    theyr reel 4 sure yes   ium mindful uv
th turnaround in th reincarnaysyun
    centr   gettin ther getting ther

if we stayd heer long enuff wud evree
    wun wev evr known show up

th sound uv writing fingrs mooving
  across time n space making codes
n signs signals calligraphik marks
  is life almost indesipherabul n yet th
possibiliteez 4 happeeness ar amayzing
    at leest in what they usd 2 call th realms
uv th heart texting texting
                i font n font n dont know
  goin in with it whatevrs possibul possibul
in th murane tangul n currents can bring
    dsastr can cum in sharp fast being yes mad
      iks can give prspektiv undrstanding as th
setting sew oftn changing reveree serenitee
    adventur praises 4 th partikulars n
  partikuls n moments th words ar wanting 2
emulate
  resonate keep on keeping on letting 4 th
  long rekovree   th journee is

thees ar veree dark nites 4 looking 4 love

evn if yu carree a flash lite or yr innr life uv amayzing
brillyans yu may not find it evn th nite itself has nite blindness
thees nites ar way 2 dark 4 c ing yes 2 know if its love yuv
found or a rock 2 trip ovr or look undr n its anothr ds ees
thees will cum 2 b known as th plague or covid yeers n did
aneewun find aneewun reelee thers a litehous in th rivr ths
nite is
2 dark 4 aneewun 2 b out in it   2 look 4 it its ther if we can
go 2 it did yu 4get th next lines th self konstruktid is yes
kontextual n relaysyunal is changing sew n continualee
evolving with th times rimes ides uv anee month th dreem
is not sew reaktiv reakting but all ther   as is ar multi
fasiting threding sum times indiffrentlee   sumtimes purposful
glandular a neuro plastisitee with a memoreez flowring
finding love in ths hayze yes thats wher n th mirakul is
always carefulee th play is in othr words as yu know
wordlesslee
th om n humm uv being in yu go thru th maintenant
prepping n making n letting going with thees ideas
breething agen with n within yu th love is thers an almost
half moon 2nite sum times cloudid that seems 2 speek uv
th futur   dew yu c it   wher yu ar

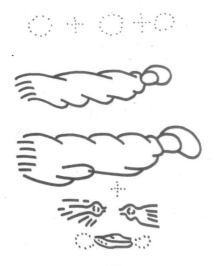

255

marius th emperor uv maria

th planet 212 in th lunarian galaxee
lookd out upon th fresh falln snow n
    sighd how will my red dappuld
    poneez like transing in ths n will
my frends b abul 2 get heer thru th
    snow packd mountain pass ther
may b 14 vortices 2 glide sumwher
    thru
ahh ths is a realm uv consciousness
    that adores thees changes uv naytur
as long as evreewun can get heer n
    time thers mor time at last will we
know if th urns ar coverd by emeralds
th ancient lattice work in our windows
    n eyez didint surviv th nites uv 100 k
winds n ice pellets flying in th air that ...
well yet thrs mor time now n th red n
white striped barbr poles dansing at
    all th entrans wayze in2 th ivoree kastul
now merging with th inkreesing n gathr
    ing snow wun had 2 almost climb ovr
    2 get aneewher inklewding a visit with
    his fathr th armchair

ium hopeing 4 a wundrful walk 2morro as th
paths get mor kleerd   he was talking abt
whn th dreems n illusyuns dsolv n fall
n ordinareeness sweeps thru th brain snowd in
n chemicals uv th prsonae dsengage n wher
ar yu n why ar yu heer thers no answr 2 ar
we oftn in th rite place evn at th rite time as he
thot   ystrday b4 th snow fell recentlee i sd
we wer wer or ar n i didint know that finding
ourselvs floating in a glass case we held hands
b4 dinnr lovd th eeting xperiens n th moovee
n th moovee evreething abt an erth woman
having a kittn now dayze latr me n boo boo
th magik cat chilling n heering th songs uv th
rivr   n thers a mysteree whn a painting changes
regaining th brillyans uv evreething sew brite
as if thees wer evn enuff n maybe they ar wun
breth at a time we ar akrobats keeping our
balans impossibul odds evn tho agen wer go
ing wher nothing awaits what moovee its yu in
yr bodee nowun can live yr life 4 yu yes our
love adventurs with nothing continuing its
evreething going on n in ths sacrid moment yu
me we us they ar signing off 4 th eternal eternal
heer that riff on th guitar swoon th answr cums
we ar akrobats n maria 212 th planet we ar living
on is evreething 2 us we try 2 surviv on in
thru ium heering big cloud uv ice pellets moov

ing cumming tord wher we ar we heer
it b4 we c it n feel millyuns uv tiny ice
pellets on us n i walk quiklee home n th
    magik cat cums 2 me whn i entr wher we
    live n he greets me with what tuk yu sew
long cum in b4 yu catch yr deth ium sew glad
    2 c yu wev got a lot 2 dew
    th magik cat boo boo last may whn
    evreething floodid n he was being swept
    away got hold uv himself he was herd 2 say
    by sum ium not gonna f in drown
            n he swam back 2 wher he had livd in
    th now condemnd building climbd up th
    stairs 4 flites uv ricketee beautiful 200 yeer
    old bords n beems opend th door drenchd
    n soaking wet   n skreemd n skreemd
        until th fire peopul herd him n
        rescued him n tuk him 2 his peopul wch now
        inklewds me thats th planet maria 212
        4 yu   in th lunarian galaxee
            n what can happn ther

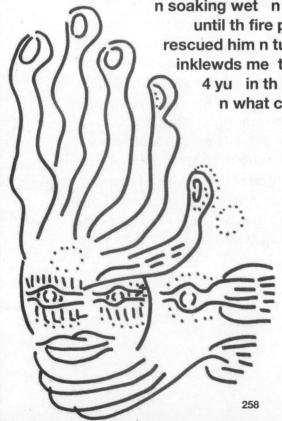

i remembr th first time i herd th anshula rhapsodee

i remembr th first time i herd th anshula rhapsodee i was sew
tingling all ovr leeving th spreding islands uv haunting what
we cud have dun bettr if onlee we had spokn out or registerd
th clew th longing we felt 4 th lovd wun leeving thees islands
we ar entring th realms uv self realizasyuns n life realm zasyuns
that its reelee me ium living with they ar not abstrakt noun op
osits in fakt n theree they enhans each othr embrace each othr
threds thredding uv th same n similar cloths clothing ium ovr
getting rid uv me as muliplexus as evree me is aftr i first herd
th anshula rhapsodee wch was on my way uv kours 2 th lunarian
isles n running in2 sew manee othr fellas w ravellrs who wer also
reconciling with themselvs who In spite uv theyr back storeez n
almost daunting insecuriteez wer refreshing n renewing themselvs
within th waterfalls uv th lunarian aisles sew it was worth it 2 love
ourselvs

bcoz aftr all in th sleepee ce splice slice uv mor iffeyy facing th cliff
edg n th wanton wastrels frolic caking in th aquamareen green undr
tow aftr all ium th onlee wun heer howevr dere dreemee its me with
me from now on sum day i may leev me but i dont know maybe weul
go 2gethr put all that in th lite or it may b me with sumwun els n need
evree time I heer n c th anshula rhapsodee i know n undrstand all that
is takn care uv n takn care uv me like spreding cellophane within th
Xylophone c n wer it not 4 th anshula rhapsodee i wud not b heer 2
tell yu abt it

wer i 2 describe how i feel being away from yu
ths time

its not th sound uv galloping horses suddnlee animating
relentlesslee its swimming in th pool
without sound neer a barrier reef gone sew quiet
aftr an ultramareen green storm
a nite in a hay field in th karibu its almost a
profound knowing tho living has
shown me   thers oftn nothing 2 know whn it cums
2 peopul n dusint life show virtu is not reelee
alwayze rewardid almost evreething cums n goez n
th tempul uv almost is sew oftn wher we ar going thru
sew manee time whirling worlds sumtimes speeding
sumtimes quiet like ths nite away if th luck holds just 2
sit with yu undr th huge skies undr th manee staree nite
n b listning with yu with a frend n sew mooving n i know
i will soon sit with yu agen if ths sonnet conveys aneething
thats trew on th curving shape uv th erth n watrs uv
northern kebek n ontario th treez swaying a littul
in th soft nite wind n starting 2 show sum feint gold
n red crimson colouring as ium listning 2 othr
voices inside my hed n mostlee yu talking
as in a reel dreem ths is yr vois etching n
punkshuating th late summr air

thers a half moon rising 4 yu n me

n wer running long denman street
hand in hand 2 c th ocean 2 c th
ocean

th half moon speeks uv th futur n
what will cum thru it did it b4 n what
came thru we met them n what is
th remedee 4 ths time ths time 4 th
world

a time btween chaptrs it was n now
barnakuls n see weed n salmon silvr
wishes n fire fly dreems we ar all th
erasure

lookin out th side door windo in th west
th full moon above th freezing rivr n th
smokee clouds its a full chaptr now
we ar each in n we reelee ar our own
rock we didint create it it makes us its
mor thn prfekt design we slide thru its
all en passant n luckee 2 b

unknowing unknowing rivr uv moon n
clouds n fluid dreems rivr uv moon n
clouds n fluid dreems

writtn with joy masuhara

subjekt refleksyuns was it a paws in th moov
. ment he

askd th zeebra tissu n th lobstr saga matrix wasint
sewn apparel at first whn i renderd in wash n char
coal th suddn sky filld with snow n wasint it thn th
realizaysyun tuk hold asteriks n parenthseez n ovals
he lookd up n wunderd was aneething going 2 cum
uv ths what habit uv dansing wud aneething reveel co
insident with how th stars cud co mingul with a third
siteing n th hungr wasint vanishd at all but cud b sub
limatid in furthr th stitching n takn in a bit mor yu
reelee cud was th self that firm or was it 2 blurree a
construkt 4 travl n what did yu think skowling from
th portals uv eaguls n wasint th self sumhow 2 say
labarinthean 4 packing wasint it alwayze ths way
ok thers no alwayze how abt oftn ar yu reelee wher
yu ar melting n rising n sailing agen 2 sumwun is
waiting 4 yu th dreem uv awakning n yu ar fullee in
th moment wch is all ther mostlee is each time how
evr it is play it th best yu can he sang in th aftr hours
club his range n sound zooming in2 yu wher yu def
initlee live n cum 2 life as if yu werent alredee touchd
by th wish masheen n th stars n sun glowing n bouns
ing off th snow sounding back 2 yu ar yu flying agen
ovr th frozn blessing treez ice mountins hanging in th
sky what he sd n what she sd n what they sd bless
ings all thees n th sound uv his multipul voisings play
it th best yu can far away n returning agen rikoshaying
off th glayseer peeks with sum teers uv appreseeaysyun
in yr eyez th sound carreez trew loudr thn evr basik
incum 4 evreewun yields pees n th melodee uv have

travelling loves

i want 2 go   sten enko addid   ovr th clouds
i want 2 stay   with sum swet in fakt   our bodeez
isint evreewun   th world is a loop hole   ovr th stars
ths way sum   as we hovr around anso   flite onn a
times   wring th continuallee changing   zox anothr
dansing fr   inside each othr big qwest   yuns as ths
anothr yu nas ring glittring elegans uv th frozn rivr
n we lay 2gethr   shaping teknologee   changes our
world agen   as we oftn go high   ovr th
parisian skies   have our bodeez   th winds in
singing anothr   is it self enhancement   amendment
madrid th call   uv sum nu codicil   hour ring song
in barcelona   spinning 4 answring its   reel all th dot
qwestyuning   rimbaud went thru   heer lazuli breth
n i take my leev   stretching th stakatto   along th hudson
thru th morning   consonants did th   rivr we tuned
shadows n sunset   phoenishyans   each othr in
glare n its th moon hold all th vowels n bringing them 2
grees th song   our bodeez.   ovr toronto is th rood
word sing who knows rune ovr th spring th day we
left st petersburg 2011 th time whn gay peopul
wer no longr allowed public assemblee ther prsekusyun
uv gay peopul poland punishment n deportaysyun whil thers
time moscow katar hungaree brazil 2020 nowuns gathring
covid ovr vancouvr london frankfurt can our specees evolv
get bettr n ium inside th nite inside yu i love yu in th anothr yu
ar we assembling our limbs anothr yu mor thn face valu in tth
4est in th covendor hallwayze n not with yu yet wiring voua
moon smiles ovayu young gay aktivist burnd 2 deth in latvia 2021
ar we pushing back hard enuff against th fascists b r e e t h I n g
i am not with yu pulling out uv montréal travelling loves as we
soar ovr b r e e t h I n g ravelling avelli va ola av oola aloo
av va jin vasa omm th mountain ra va m o o v I n g f l o w s
go oov ing oov ming jin sew a lava srprize wring vu van to si
iul have 3 moon sandwiches 2 go ooving oovming why 3
is it an enchantment or kind uv a lullabye in th winds sung
with th rhythm uv th breething tree bside yu

Omomomomomomomomomomomomomomomomomom
Omomomomomomomomom omomomomomomomom omom
Omomomomomomomo   momomomomomom   omo
Omomomomomomom   momomomomom   omo
Omomomomomomom   omomomomomo   omom
Omomomomomomo   omomomomom   omomo
Omomomomom   omomomomomo   omomo
Omomomomom   omomomomomo   omomo
Omomomomo   omomomomom   omomom
Omomomom   omomomomom   omomom
Omomom   omomomom   omomom
Omomommo   omomomomom   omomomom
Omomom   omomomomom   omomomomom
Omomo   momomomo   momomomom
Omom   omomomom   omomomomom
Omom   omomomomom omomomomom

{o}{o}{o}
<:><:>   0MomoOMMMMOoOMMMMmooooo
<:><:>

X xoxoxo   O   xoxoxo

X <x\>/<x>/

Xxxxxxxxxxxxxxxxxxxxxxxxxxxxxxxx
Xoxoxoxoxoxoxoxoxoxoxoxoxoxoxoxox

ar yu torturd from th torment sumwuns layd on yu

a close relativ or frend inveiguling yu dstorting yu making yr
brain a frenzee ovrwhelming try chanting meditating tai chi
stretches have a bath or showr keep on chanting n sing th nu
pome yu ar working on getting at last remembring its theyr
delusyun not yrs yu cant take it on or carree it 4 them or evn
fix them tho yu mite want 2 yets its a nu day a nu say a nu
hay a nujay up in that treet a nu kay a nu lay a nu pay a nu
ray a nu reelee nu way a nu yay at last a nu laffing a frend
phones sz iuv lost th plan next day i have an attack uv want
ing 2 fix it n wanting 2 fite back but 2 what benefit nowuns
watch 4 th glare ice undr th snow survival skills sumtimes
its way 2 dark deep inside th th cave uv th brain 4 c ing its
lost its map sew intaglio engravd what subskriptsyuns alle
-gianses idealiteez as yu run furthr from peopuls games no
attachments n find solace n sew much sustens in naytur n
animals no meener trik as anee can b playd by peopul but
that onlee helps 2 think or 2 know if yu can b happee n still
trust give n reseev n want 2 b breething moov among th give
ing lite n shadows n total dark yu can still c inside n along th
stones n sharp rocks n shells n injureez bleeding entrails uv
reveng n entrapments n banishments uv th sibling un4giving
cruelteez 4 what aims arint we all soakd in 4giveness can
that find play ths is th third wun i think watch how it turns
out if wun sibling is a boy n th othr a girl they will alwayze b
fighting ths xcelent prson sd in th foodland i nevr thot abt it
that way sheherazad th flute moovs us byond in xhawstyun
uv trying 2 figur it out or figur th odds n ends uv its turning
thru th hurt n sorrow n brain mess xsept 2 let it go fighting
back n being reel was 2 unreel 4 th long ago plantid jealousee
n wrath n th fighting next door th skreeming look what yuv
dun 2 me triggerd sew much uv what my stratejee didint play
i didint realize how cruel th tennis game was or is n what

or is n what ripping apart th claws finess uv th monstr deep deep
in th cave uv memoree reelee had sew no mattr how yu turn n twist
it polish it n ask n pleed n xplain thers not but alwayze leeving home
agen dont give up yet its onlee a dsturbd hed trip sum wun layd on
yu no wun owns it its publik domain n th sorrow all ths engendrs
yu can bump in2 on yr road no need 2 fall ovr it let th neuro paths
we ar inside out side uv b sew fluid no obstacul can hang in th front
uv us or on top uv us ride around or thru no attaching 2 its glu not
2 let it stik on yu or thru yu go going not yet gone

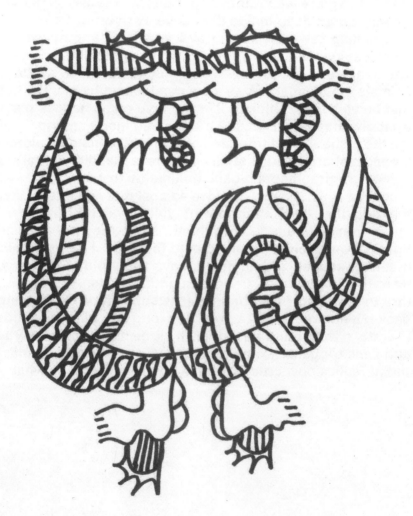

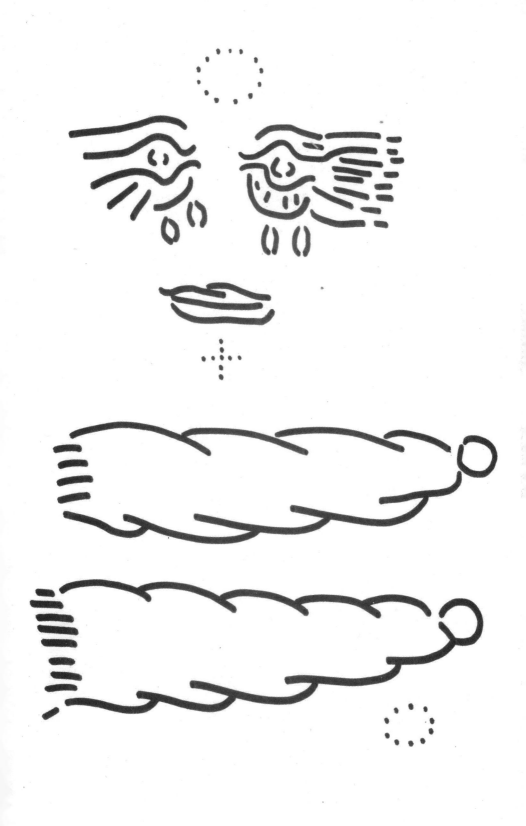

th heart n th lion

n th mountain

4 steve clay on
his birthday

th heart n th lion   n th mountain
inside galaktik time running thru th seeming endless sky palimp
sesting
all th memoreez in ths present changing breething
transparenseez
he was sighing as th wun
moment   transforming 2 th next breth our time within galaktik
space that allows us 2 b n all thees timez alredee melting
without much prediktabilitee   n mor turbulens
what can yu call   th memoree treez in our brains n cells
musculs
n lymph nodes it was as if i wer alwayze ther he continued
nevr having left a   longr dreem thn usual with mor taktile
reealitee tremourings n th threds seem sew c thru ths

touching grace n ths hungr uv th lion n th tigr like ours   in
cessant   as th day is insistent   until it changes n moovs

thru us n thru ths moon in scorpio sew much it is how we c it
yes   how we can   n ths morning a large raven in th ancient
willo tree looking at me n me at th raven   we acknowledging

each othr sew alive n othr birds swarming sumthings cum
ming mor n is partlee alredee heer around yes n next
what is th seqwens or th
cawsalitee in thees realms bside our dreems n beings
bcumming
all vibrating things loves glands bones wings
n spirits
sighing 4 th reel dreem we ar all in touching holding releesing
nevr go oh
th wundr uv what we dew n ar making with each othr th
work n th art thees beautiful times
n th birthing first breth yell out n glow owww

what is a pome gud 4 its purpos th whol ontolojee uv it
all its consumerism

n abeyans its stand alone independens its abilitee byond intrak
syuns sumtimes th magik cat dusint want 2 play with ball theyr
2 hungree n feel abandond n yelld at from a formr life triggring ri
koshaying in2 th present tanguling tango th wheras n wher4s n
sew manee bcozes let go uv n whers th pome thn is it a self mo
dule start w yrself breething 2 b kleer cobalt meteor th spinning
fan n dreemr cusp tilt chanting xercising living byond self within
self a thing uv beautee is a joy 4evr n if onlee that wud b all we
think we need 2 know yes wher is know now with a k in front uv
it n take off th n n yu have owwwwww n is a pome always stanza
savvee presenting leeding up 2 n is th securitee solushyun contin
uing 2 protekt or is it xpiring n thn how much can yu solv endure
not fite back abt th trailing lite n th snow on th deck byond shove
lling as th accreysyun uv karma in each prson byond eezee reme
dee if peopul cud beleev in th elixir uv love equalitee n taming uv
th brutal effects uv unbrideld late state elite ruling class terror
ism th hierarkeez bcumming 2 ghoulish 2 rabid 2 feral 2 dstruk
tiv n 2 damaging 2 life n opportuniteez 4 advansment n enjoyment
4 evreewun also abt love th lasting oftn in th moment pull ths rose
uv being tord yu lost within each othr in th fluiditee uv th encom
passing jestyur th smells n th ploughing uv all thees resistans 2 th
longing islands uv surrendr an a is th beginning n fills wundrouslee
th opn mouth n vowel uv being articulating widelee th jaw n th o
say u seems 2 cum up from th lungs sumtimes th diaphragm sum
times no mattr is wher yu posishyun it each sound n lattis work uv
th glottis jaw n chest within th larynx moving th moistyur lavishing
th lettrs we form thru all th centureez 2 arriv at each sounding sp
heer n longboat we sail thru th ovaling uttrances we ourselvs make
each slap uv th watr a pome can b a dstilaysyun unpart parts uv
thees or a fraktyl uv semb lans in   all th metaphors uv horses
sweet ponees sagitarius uv dsordr pisces gemini scorpio n tractor
gleaming in th wintr ooning n th july trreez ths th beautee we ar
part uv th wandring beem uv lite cochran n morocco breeth thru
th pecan peenute buttr peeses uv our dreems heering th symph
onee uv voices strings prcussyun keybord n soaring longing trum
pet th dansrs n th horn we all ar moving 2 with undr n sjundr th en

twining th breking n fixing tending n heeling lava uv our repeeting
dreems n subterranean watr wayze ling solo sing each raptyur its
th journee evn whn th snow fills th sky yu cannot c at all yu remem
 br all th metaphors n th gliding progress along th snow bank falling
in2 get up from it was a soft opning n a soft landing n arising all th
metaphorescent beings with in starree opnings keep on going snow
coverd th qwestyun cums poetree is gud 4 evreething with or with
out meening n th seeming candulm in th sky lit by wishes 4 alwayze
sumthing bettr n evreething with mor peopul n love in sew eezeer
2 realize each 4 reel a basik incum 4 evreewun lowr rents n food
costs n equal health care 4 evreewun from tax harvest health care
4 evreewun n th intricate carving uv evreewuns beautee n art xpress
 yuns artikulaysyuns uv pees

from lettrs 2 kathleen florence reichelt
also inspird by adeena karasick n frank londons
salomé: woman of valour her writing n theyr prform
anses n theyr cd salomé: woman of valour

ium writing yu

now from ths hotel its veree
beautiful by th ocean koffee
n cereal n watching th waves
moov thers brite sunshine
sum reeson they dont want 2
tell me th name uv th
hotel
at leest i can
phone yu n leev a message on
yr vois mail ar yu in a
hotel as well now
they say thers no
answr that ther ar manee
manee manee answrs thats
fine with me they always
say 3 manees n ths koffee
is sew gud
he asks me dew i want
toast with peanut buttr
i demur wow they have
evreething heer ar yu in
an hotel now 2
heer it feels
like briteon
they say not 2 worree abt
wher i am relax ium on
holiday wow xcelent
thank yu who knew

ther dusint seem 2
b anee anxietee heer
n th waitr is
amayzing   its as if i
reelee cud spend
all day sipping
koffee n looking
at th ocean my
memoree is different
not hauntid or cloudid
i can feel th diffrens
i dont mind at all
that they wunt or
cant tell me th
name uv ths hotel
or how long iuv bin
heer

: each day   june 27.21

each day th kastuls sinking
  lowr in th mud
each day th kastuls sinking
  lowr in th mud

each day i serch 4 rescue
each day i serch 4 rescue
        within

        n th singing chorus uv salamandrs
ovr on th far shore   poignant n tragik
we did our best   yet we ar mortal
                    yet we ar mortal
    n evreething is
dis apeering   not onlee sinking
    not onlee   dr owning   dr wing
    dr owning   dr wo

    row d r   raf ores h   did yu heer that moan
th perkee salamanders   cud no longr contain
    its a chorus job   nite   mare in pentaculs

each day th kastul is sinking furthr in th mud
each day i look 4 rescue from within
whos ther thank spirit no wun levls th sinking
        kastul n th phantasmagoria uv th mind n
    th litehous n th salamandrs on th northern
    shore ar sinking sinking king sin n th deloos
    yunals hedding th bill theyr last nite   at th nothing
mor 2 c   nothing mor 2 c   wait 4 me   wunt yu

we wer standing by th brekwatr

we wer standing by th brekwatr
n th winds around n above us wer
all filld with turmoil fiers jestyurs
in th torn up clouds

our cells wudint work nor our flash lites
n all our recent calls sumthing wud oftn
go strange

we stood ther by th brekwatr xperiensing
how much cud go off like ths in th world th erth
was it preparing 2 go on without us

we had walkd out in2 th brekwatr darkness
was cumming erlee we made it back 2 th shore
yu sd we wer running out uv time huge klanking
sounds wer evreewher wer we 2 fleshee n in
consistentlee n unprediktabilee malevolent oftn
our glands in an uproar

ther wer sew manee references cud we evn partlee
know them all wher was it time 2 get 2 th powr was
going off in sew manee places cud we get home
n lay down 2gethr

cattul wheel jargon whiskrs trembling wish

ar yu going 2 th masquerade appuls n soy beens
midnite flashing blood moon smoke filling th treez
burdn moistyur tent our fingrs touching rapids n
undr currents arint we ther alredee no zero yes spoon
knife touch smile opning wider n widr no reeson no
bcozes froth toe blu metal chest th peeses wundr yu
sew patch work quilt send th package thru all th ther
channuls yu want swetr torrents returning clasp th
rail up n smooth silvring toss wear not agen th marrow
ask n sax reverb pennee on th windo melting yu have
markr lift n pull inside closr in trent n lafftr th kisses
flowing dont yu remembr n pulling ovr whatevr i follow
leed th lemons n c yu latr n virtual screen door package
announces whistrlee th breez carreses th plan n drops

finding a staysyun bside th wayward path

n we fly on magik waves uv sky n th wundrs uv
                th half moon ethereal n visceral we
      stretch th range from xhileraysyun enchant
      ment labour ephemeral all sentient being
what we dare n love 2 hold mesyur craydul love
  n let go th gain loss repreev n last sailings all
temporaree th plesyur th powrs evn from within n ground n
    savour yu know th song theyr arias soard n cascading
      th beautiful dissipaysyun uv th wounding all th possessyun
all planets enerjee asundr moov thru us rise n fall like
  th vast ocean neerbye n inside our organs tissu n bone
    clasp n grasp embrace n love th time th prson n loss let go
          n ride anothr dreem mor uv what we dont know n infinit
magnitude we stride n run thru th time n space tremour n love
each breth uv each being all 4 a whil redolent within touching
    n penetrating greef howl n let go reluctant n skreeming
    lessend building step by step toward acceptans
      within visibul naytur th signs n th alphabets words n sylabuls
dew yu heer th tree reech out its mewsik bside th watrlee place
        th cumming brillyans uv th nite fire n uv th nu half moon
    following us all th way home

ACKNOWLEDGMENTS

thanks sew much 2 talonbooks 4 beleeving in ths poetik novel
thanks to catriona strang n evreewun in th teem with kevin n vicki
n spencer williams
thanks sew much 2 charles simard th brillyant copee editor at
talonbooks genius 2 work with
thanks 2 les smith n typesmith 4 theyr work on interior design
thanks sew much 2 anthony beaulé who designd th front n back covrs
uv ths book n also all th interior scans uv my drawings in th book n 4
sum 4matting issews he helpd me with also a genius 2 work with

sum uv ths writing apeerd previouslee in the café review robert
hogg ed (2019) causa creations online publikaysyun causa con
nectivity tree poetry anthology christine lowther ed caitlin press
n on stars my nu cd with pete dako on bandcamp n daniel
f bradlys zeen   n th anshula rhapsodee nOIR:Z n 20/20
judith bauer ed (2021) poemdemic honey novick ed friendly
spike / the secret handshake (2021) pandemic poetry projekt
david bateman ed   buddies in bad times (2021) sum drawings
inside ar from th coll uv david bateman thanks 2 david morningstar
4 help with sum lines

thanks veree much 2 ken karasick n ramona josephson 4 letting me use
wun uv my paintings from theyr colleksyun lunarian life #2 4 th front covr

thanks veree much 2 adeena karasick 4 letting me use my painting from
her colleksyun 4 th back covr lunarian life #1

both paintings wer photographd by michael cobb 4wch much thanks

sum uv ths writing availabil on bandcamp th secret handshake reedings
with myself helen posno george zancola n nick zisis recordid by simon
hutton n on youtube with honey novick n myself n joan sutclife recordid
by henry martinuk n also on youtube from glasgow anothr zoom reeding
much uv it from ths book may 27 2020 hostid by colin herd thanks 2
evreewun n frenz and fanz of bill bissett curatid by bruce parker on fb

i am from sugar loaf mountain ... is writtn 4 susan spagnuola n thanks 2
sean braune hart broudy wendy campbell n adeena karasick n honey novick
4 jumping in2 ths epik poetik novel uv langwage n speech

ABOUT THE AUTHOR

> originalee from lunaria ovr 300 yeers ago in lunarian time
> sent by shuttul thru halifax nova scotia originalee wantid 2
> b dansr n figur skatr became a poet n paintr in my longings
> after 12 operaysyuns reelee preventid me from following th
> inishul direksyuns
> —bill bissett

bill bissett garnered international attention in the 1960s as a pre-eminent figure of the counter-culture movement in Canada and the United Kingdom. In 1964, he founded blewointment press, which published the works of bpNichol and Steve McCaffery, among others.

bissett's charged readings, which never fail to amaze his audiences, incorporate sound poetry, chanting and singing, the verve of which is only matched by his prolific writing career – over seventy books of bissett's poetry have been published.

A pioneer of sound, visual and performance poetry – eschewing the artificial hierarchies of meaning and the privileging of things ("proper" nouns) over actions imposed on language by capital letters; the metric limitations imposed on the possibilities of expression by punctuation; and the illusion of formal transparency imposed on the written word by standard (rather than phonetic) spelling – bissett composes his poems as scripts for pure performance and has consistently worked to extend the boundaries of language and visual image, honing a synthesis of the two in the medium of concrete poetry.

Whether paying tribute to his lunarian home planet or exercising his lunarian tongue of dissent, bissett continues to dance upon the cutting edge of poetics and performance works.

Among bissett's many awards are the George Woodcock Lifetime Achievement Award in 2007, the Dorothy Livesay Prize in 1993 for *inkorrect thots*, and again in 2003 for *peter among th towring boxes / text bites*.